SECUNDUM COR TUUM

I0835343

Raymond Leo Cardinal Burke

NOVENA & CONSECRATION
to Our Lady of Guadalupe
for NINE DAYS OR NINE MONTHS

The Shrine of Our Lady of Guadalupe publishes works of prayer, catechesis, and Christian reflection in service of the mission of the Shrine and the life of the Church. Rooted in pilgrimage and devotion to Our Lady of Guadalupe and her immaculate Heart, and to the Sacred Heart of Jesus, these publications seek to foster faith, deepen love for Christ, and support the faithful in living the truths of the Catholic faith.

ISBN: 978-1-963716-02-3

Learn more about the Shrine of Our Lady of Guadalupe at

guadalupeshrine.org

Author
Raymond Leo Cardinal Burke

Publisher
Becket Ghioto

Design Consultants
Megan Pilcher
Molly Brown

Copyeditors
Sarah Greydanus
Molly Hostetler

Nican Mopohua Translation
Anderson, Carl A., and Eduardo Chávez. *Our Lady of Guadalupe: Mother of the Civilization of Love.* New York: Doubleday, 2009.

TABLE of CONTENTS

SECUNDUM COR TUUM

Por devocion de Dn. Juan Baptista Eche
uerria.

INTRODUCTION

"Am I not here, I who am your Mother?
Are you not under my protection?"

—Our Lady of Guadalupe
to Saint Juan Diego

These words spoken to Saint Juan Diego transcend time through the maternal love of Our Lady of Guadalupe, represented by her miraculous image on the tilma of Saint Juan Diego. When there was much darkness and confusion within Mexico, Our Lady appeared to him as a loving and merciful mother.

The world in which Saint Juan Diego lived 500 years ago does not seem dissimilar from ours today. Famine and disease were rampant then. War in the Holy Land threatened to collapse that beautiful and tortured region into chaos. Pernicious error and confusion within the Church about the most fundamental truths taught by God through human reason and faith corroded the virtues of the faithful. It might have seemed to many that all hope was lost.

During that time, when Our Lady of Guadalupe first appeared to Saint Juan Diego, he had the profound sense that, in some way, Heaven had come to earth. Through his conversations with Our Lady and his obedience in carrying out her will, his life was changed forever. It was Our Lady, or, rather, the Child in her womb, who had transformed his ordinary world and made it extraordinary: God was present in his midst. In time, Our Lady claimed the New World for Christ, drawing over nine million new souls into the Church by the time of Saint Juan Diego's death in 1548.

At this time in history, when we again witness much darkness and confusion concerning the most fundamental truths about human life and its source in the love of marriage, we are ever more in need of Our Lady of Guadalupe to intercede for our nation and for our world.

The spirit of the world, the author of the culture of death, would have us believe that weakness and sinfulness can bring us happiness and freedom, when, in truth, they bring despair and captivity.

Today, we hope for that same grace of conversion from our sins. Today, we pray for the same transformation of a culture of death to a culture of life and divine love. Today, we seek Our Lady's maternal love and protection, which she offers to anyone who seeks her Divine Son through her intercession.

To that end, in 2024, I called upon all Catholics, especially those in the Americas, to join me in praying a Nine-Month novena seeking Our Lady's intercession. Thanks be to God, nearly 190,000 of the faithful answered the call! This immense spiritual undertaking began on March 12th and culminated in a consecration to Our Lady of Guadalupe on December 12th, her Solemnity. Those who signed up for this cause received short video reflections from me each month to help guide them during this vital spiritual work, in addition to regular written reflections and prayers.

It was a tremendous opportunity to do something transformative and powerful—for our nation, for our Church, and for our own lives—and it remains a tremendous opportunity still to this day.

With this book, you, too, can pray a Nine-Day or Nine-Month Novena to Our Lady of Guadalupe. Inside this book are the Novena Prayer, the Novena Reflections, the Act of Consecration, and the Daily Consecration to Our Lady of Guadalupe. Bear in mind that the Act of Consecration to Our Lady of Guadalupe is prayed once per year on December 12th, Our Lady's Solemnity. The Daily Prayer is to be offered at the beginning of each day, as a way of living the Consecration to Our Lady of Guadalupe faithfully, every day of our lives. It is only through prayer, devotion, and sacred worship, that we obtain the grace of thinking, speaking, and acting according to the Mind and Heart of Christ.

The damage sin causes can seem so great. But take heart! Evil cannot approach the power of God's grace. Sin cannot prevent His healing mercy from finding those who repent and seek it. And nothing can diminish the love of Our Lady, whose maternal care and protection for us remains as strong today as it was 500 years ago.

Raymond Leo Cardinal Burke

Raymond Leo Cardinal Burke

HOW TO MAKE
the NOVENA & CONSECRATION *to* OUR LADY *of* GUADALUPE

Pray the Novena Prayer to Our Lady of Guadalupe for all nine days if you have committed to the Nine-Day Novena beginning on December 3rd and ending on December 12th, or, if you have committed to the Nine-Month Novena, pray the Novena Prayer to Our Lady of Guadalupe every day, beginning on March 12th and ending on December 12th.

On December 12th, make a pilgrimage to your local church and, before Our Eucharistic Lord reserved in the tabernacle, pray the Act of Consecration to Our Lady of Guadalupe. While the act of a pilgrimage is a significant testimony of your commitment to be consecrated to Our Lady of Guadalupe, if one cannot be made, then pray the Act of Consecration with your whole heart at a place that is most convenient to you, whether that be at home, or in your room, or anyplace that will afford your soul the greatest spiritual benefit. Although a priest does not need to be present for the validity of your consecration, nevertheless, receiving a blessing from a priest, especially on the Solemnity of Our Lady of Guadalupe, on the official consecration day, always ushers forth grace and spiritual fruit. The Act of Consecration to Our Lady of Guadalupe is prayed once on December 12th.

On December 13th, the day after you make the Act of Consecration to Our Lady of Guadalupe, begin praying the Daily Consecration to Our Lady of Guadalupe at the beginning of each day. It is the first way of living the

Consecration to Our Lady of Guadalupe faithfully, every day of our lives, and is our way of remaining always within the mantle of Our Lady, secure in her maternal embrace. If you are praying the Nine-Day Novena to Our Lady of Guadalupe, pray the Daily Consecration Prayer every day until December 2nd; conclude praying the Daily Consecration Prayer; and begin praying the Novena Prayer to Our Lady of Guadalupe on December 3rd through December 11th. If you are praying the Nine-Month Novena, conclude praying the Daily Consecration Prayer on March 11th and begin praying the Novena Prayer to Our Lady of Guadalupe on March 12th every day of the nine months until December 11th. Whether praying the Novena Prayer for nine days or for nine months, conclude the Novena Prayer on December 11th and pray the Act of Consecration to Our Lady of Guadalupe on December 12th and then begin praying again the Daily Consecration Prayer to Our Lady of Guadalupe on December 13th.

OUTLINE

Daily Novena

December 3 through December 11, pray: *Novena Prayer*

December 12, pray: *Act of Consecration Prayer*

December 13 though that year to December 2 of the following year, pray: *Daily Consecration Prayer*

Nine Month Novena

First month

March 12: *read Reflection One, pray Novena Prayer*
March 24: *read Reflection Two, pray Novena Prayer*

Second month

April 12: *read Reflection One, pray Novena Prayer*
April 24: *read Reflection Two, pray Novena Prayer*

Third month

May 12: *read Reflection One, pray Novena Prayer*
May 24: *read Reflection Two, pray Novena Prayer*

Fourth month

June 12: *read Reflection One, pray Novena Prayer*
June 24: *read Reflection Two, pray Novena Prayer*

Fifth month

July 12: *read Reflection One, pray Novena Prayer*
July 24: *read Reflection Two, pray Novena Prayer*

Six month

August 12: *read Reflection One, pray Novena Prayer*
August 24: *read Reflection Two, pray Novena Prayer*

Seventh month

September 12: *read Reflection One, pray Novena Prayer*
September 24: *read Reflection Two, pray Novena Prayer*

Eighth month

November 12: *read Reflection One, pray Novena Prayer*
November 24: *read Reflection Two, pray Novena Prayer*

Ninth month

December 12: *read Reflection, pray Act of Consecration Prayer*

Daily Consecration

December 13 though that year to March 11 of the following year, pray: *Daily Consecration Prayer*

To view the videos, go to link or QR code below:
novena.cardinalburke.com/novena/reflections-library

NINE DAY NOVENA
to Our Lady *of* Guadalupe

DAY ONE

Today, we begin our Nine-Day Novena to Our Lady of Guadalupe.

Our Lady of Guadalupe first appeared to Saint Juan Diego just before dawn on a Saturday morning, December 9, 1531. Although the home of Juan Diego was in Cuauhtitlán, his spiritual home was Tlatelolco, the place of his baptism and of his ongoing instruction in the Catholic faith. Our Lady favored with her apparition and chose as her messenger a humble Christian who was seeking to deepen his knowledge of the faith through instruction from the priest whom he identifies as an image of Christ alive for us in the Church.

When Our Lady began to speak with him, she immediately declared the truth of her being, of her relationship with God as Mother of God the Son Incarnate, and of her relationship with Juan Diego, as with all Christians. She declared:

> Know, know for sure my dearest and youngest son, that I am truly the ever perfect Holy Virgin Mary, who has the honor to be Mother of the one true God for whom we all live, the Creator of people, the Lord of all around us and of what is close to us, the Lord of Heaven, the Lord of Earth (*Nican Mopohua*, no. 26).

What is primary for Our Lady in her relationship with Juan Diego and in his collaboration as her messenger is the truth that she is the Virgin Mother of God the Son Incarnate Who is the King of Heaven and Earth and Who alone is our salvation.

The first lesson which Our Lady of Guadalupe teaches us to equip us for today's grave crisis is the inseparable unity of truth and love. We cannot truly love another person while also disregarding or betraying the truth which should inform every relationship. The fundamental approach to the crisis of the family, of society, and of the Church is the knowledge of truth and the practice of it with love.

NOVENA PRAYER *to* Our Lady *of* Guadalupe

O Virgin Mother of God, we fly to your protection and beg your intercession against the darkness and sin which ever more envelop the world and menace the Church. Your Son, Our Lord Jesus Christ, gave you to us as our mother as He died on the Cross for our salvation. So, too, in 1531, when darkness and sin beset us, He sent you, as Our Lady of Guadalupe, on Tepeyac to lead us to Him Who alone is our light and our salvation.

Through your apparitions on Tepeyac and your abiding presence with us on the miraculous mantle of your messenger, Saint Juan Diego, millions of souls converted to faith in your Divine Son. Through this novena and our consecration to you, we humbly implore your intercession for our daily conversion of life to Him and the conversion of millions more who do not yet believe in Him. In our homes and in our nation, lead us to Him Who alone wins the victory over sin and darkness in us and in the world.

Unite our hearts to your Immaculate Heart so that they may find their true and lasting home in the Most Sacred Heart of Jesus. Ever guide us along the pilgrimage of life to our eternal home with Him. So may our hearts, one with yours, always trust in God's promise of salvation, in His never-failing mercy toward all who turn to Him with a humble and contrite heart. Through this novena and our consecration to you, O Virgin of Guadalupe, lead all souls in America and throughout the world to your Divine Son in Whose name we pray. Amen.

DAY TWO

As our second day of the Nine-Day Novena begins, some of us may be experiencing the worst temptations from Satan to surrender and stop praying the Novena Prayer every day. Throughout the days of the apparitions, Saint Juan Diego was subject to the temptations of Satan, who placed in him the doubt that he was worthy and capable of carrying out the directions and orders of the Heavenly Queen. After his first visit to the Bishop, he was convinced that only someone of higher social status could carry out Our Lady's mission. In a rather eloquent way, he described his own lowliness to the Virgin Mother of God:

> So I beg you, my Lady, my Queen, my little Girl, to have one of the nobles who are held in esteem, one who is known, respected, honored, have him carry on, take your venerable breath, your venerable word, so that he will be believed. Because I am really just a man from the country, I'm the porter's rope, I'm a back frame, just a tail, a wing; I myself need to be led, carried on someone's back; there, where you sent me, it is not my place to go or to stay, my little Girl, my littlest Daughter, my Lady, my Girl. Please, excuse me, I will afflict your face, your heart; I will fall into your anger, your displeasure, my Lady Mistress (*Nican Mopohua*, nos. 54-56).

But the Mother of God, the Mother of Divine Grace, responded by confirming him as her messenger, assuring him that he, too, was called to carry out the mission of bringing God Incarnate to the world, to his brothers and sisters.

Our Lady of Guadalupe assured him that she has many upon whom to call for the mission of her messenger, but that Juan Diego has been called and, therefore, must trust that he can carry out the mission. She replies to him:

> Listen my youngest son, know for sure that I have no lack of servants, of messengers, to whom I can give the task of carrying my breath, my word, so that they carry out my will; but it is necessary that you, personally, go and plead, that by your intercession, my wish, my will, become a reality. And I beg you, my youngest son, and I strictly order you, to go again tomorrow to see the Bishop. And in my name, make him know, make him hear my wish, my will, so that he will bring into being, he will build, my sacred house that I ask of him. And carefully tell him again how I, personally, the ever Virgin Holy Mary, I, who am the Mother of God, sent you as my messenger (*Nican Mopohua*, nos. 58-62).

In the battle for the truth, we must never give way to discouragement which is always the first temptation of the devil. When we are tempted to be discouraged or to be defeated, let us recall the vision of the final victory of Christ's Redemptive Incarnation, recounted in the Book of Revelation. In the vision, Satan is determined to destroy the "woman clothed with the sun" (Rv 12, 1) and her Son. But the Divine Son of Mary is "caught up to God and to his throne" (Rv 12, 5). Thus, He brings his victory over sin and death to its fullness. In fact, the image of the Virgin of Guadalupe which God left for us on the tilma (mantle) of Saint Juan Diego is the "woman clothed with the sun" who carries in her womb the Savior of the world.

Our Lady's motherly words to Saint Juan Diego speak to us, too, as they reflect a fundamental truth of the faith: Christ's dwelling with us in His holy Church, the Indwelling of the Holy Spirit in our souls, enables even the weakest person to carry out God's will with heroic virtue. Only with the aid of God's grace, through the intercession of Our Lady, Mediatrix of All Graces, will we persevere in this Novena and Consecration.

NOVENA PRAYER *to* Our Lady *of* Guadalupe

O Virgin Mother of God, we fly to your protection and beg your intercession against the darkness and sin which ever more envelop the world and menace the Church. Your Son, Our Lord Jesus Christ, gave you to us as our mother as He died on the Cross for our salvation. So, too, in 1531, when darkness and sin beset us, He sent you, as Our Lady of Guadalupe, on Tepeyac to lead us to Him Who alone is our light and our salvation.

Through your apparitions on Tepeyac and your abiding presence with us on the miraculous mantle of your messenger, Saint Juan Diego, millions of souls converted to faith in your Divine Son. Through this novena and our consecration to you, we humbly implore your intercession for our daily conversion of life to Him and the conversion of millions more who do not yet believe in Him. In our homes and in our nation, lead us to Him Who alone wins the victory over sin and darkness in us and in the world.

Unite our hearts to your Immaculate Heart so that they may find their true and lasting home in the Most Sacred Heart of Jesus. Ever guide us along the pilgrimage of life to our eternal home with Him. So may our hearts, one with yours, always trust in God's promise of salvation, in His never-failing mercy toward all who turn to Him with a humble and contrite heart. Through this novena and our consecration to you, O Virgin of Guadalupe, lead all souls in America and throughout the world to your Divine Son in Whose name we pray. Amen.

DAY THREE

As we officially begin the third day of our Nine-Day Novena, let us thank God and Our Lady for the grace of perseverance which Our Lord, through the maternal mediation of Our Lady, has given to us so that we might fight the good fight, finish the race, and keep the Faith (cf. 2 Tim. 4, 7).

Our Lady commissioned Saint Juan Diego to be her heroic messenger, just as she commissions us today to lead others to Christ by handing on to them the truths of the Faith and its beauty in the life of prayer and, above all, of divine worship. However, after Bishop Juan de Zumárraga's initial skeptical reaction to Saint Juan Diego's account of Our Lady's desire, Saint Juan Diego considered himself to be unworthy of the mission that the Mother of God had entrusted into his hands. Saint Juan Diego was always docile and obedient, but, at the same time, he doubted that he could do all that God was asking of him. When the work seemed particularly difficult, he thought of reasons why the mission should be entrusted to someone else, and he even suggested to Our Lady that he was not the right person for her mission. Yet as a child is comforted by a mother's love, so too, Saint Juan Diego found comfort in Our Lady's words:

> I will reward the care, the work and the fatigue that you have put into this for me (*Nican Mopohua*, no. 92).

Our Lord Himself teaches us that God reveals His will to the "childlike" (Mt 11, 25), to those who, like Him, are "meek and humble of heart" (Mt 11, 29), to those who recognize that all that they are and have comes from the hand of God and who, therefore, place all their trust in Him. He assures us that, if doing His will demands much labor and is burdensome, He will "give [us] rest" (Mt 11, 28). Using an image from farming to describe our work with Him for the salvation of the world, he encourages to "take [His] yoke" (Mt 11, 29) upon our shoulders. He declares: "For my yoke is easy, and my burden light" (Mt 11, 30).

In our daily struggle to be faithful and generous co-workers with Christ in His saving work, let us call upon the intercession of Our Lady of Guadalupe and her heroic messenger, Saint Juan Diego, even as we seek to follow their example. Christ will never fail us. He will render efficacious for our salvation and the salvation of the world our every good thought, word, and deed. When we are tempted to give up in the battle, let us bear in mind Our Lady's words to Saint Juan Diego for they are motherly words which will comfort and encourage us as well: "I will reward the care, the work and the fatigue that you have put into this for me."

NOVENA PRAYER *to* Our Lady *of* Guadalupe

O Virgin Mother of God, we fly to your protection and beg your intercession against the darkness and sin which ever more envelop the world and menace the Church. Your Son, Our Lord Jesus Christ, gave you to us as our mother as He died on the Cross for our salvation. So, too, in 1531, when darkness and sin beset us, He sent you, as Our Lady of Guadalupe, on Tepeyac to lead us to Him Who alone is our light and our salvation.

Through your apparitions on Tepeyac and your abiding presence with us on the miraculous mantle of your messenger, Saint Juan Diego, millions of souls converted to faith in your Divine Son. Through this novena and our consecration to you, we humbly implore your intercession for our daily conversion of life to Him and the conversion of millions more who do not yet believe in Him. In our homes and in our nation, lead us to Him Who alone wins the victory over sin and darkness in us and in the world.

Unite our hearts to your Immaculate Heart so that they may find their true and lasting home in the Most Sacred Heart of Jesus. Ever guide us along the pilgrimage of life to our eternal home with Him. So may our hearts, one with yours, always trust in God's promise of salvation, in His never-failing mercy toward all who turn to Him with a humble and contrite heart. Through this novena and our consecration to you, O Virgin of Guadalupe, lead all souls in America and throughout the world to your Divine Son in Whose name we pray. Amen.

DAY FOUR

Great are the difficulties we are called to face in the Church and in the world. When such difficulties seem overwhelming, even prayer may appear to be one more difficulty, but that is a snare of Satan. The truth is that prayer, which is a union of our hearts with the glorious-pierced Heart of Jesus, is the balm of healing and strength in bearing all our burdens. The great test of our total dedication to the mission that we have taken up is to persevere as we pray for the conversion of the world.

The great test of Saint Juan Diego's total dedication to Our Lady came with the grave illness of his uncle, Juan Bernardino. It was after the second apparition on December 10th, during which Our Lady requested that he return the next day, December 11th, to receive from her the proof of the truth of the apparitions, which Bishop Juan de Zumárraga was requesting. He found his uncle mortally ill. He, therefore, remained at home with him for the entire day on December 11th. Early in the morning of December 12th, he was going to ask the priest to come to prepare his uncle for death. In order to prevent any delay in obtaining critical spiritual help for his dying uncle, he attempted to avoid an encounter with Our Lady. She, however, saw him and approached him, inquiring of his plans.

Saint Juan Diego explained the grave situation of his uncle to which he was attending, but, at the same time, he assured Our Lady that, as soon as the spiritual needs of his uncle had been met, he would return to complete the mission which she had entrusted to him.

In response, Our Lady reassured him that his uncle was already well. In fact, at the exact moment, just as she appeared to Saint Juan Diego, she also appeared to Juan Bernardino, and she healed him of his illness. Our Lady's words of comfort to Juan Diego are words that should comfort us as well whenever we experience the temptation to doubt the importance and immediacy of carrying out all that Our Lady desires and has asked of us.

> Listen, put it into your heart, my youngest son, that what frightened you, what afflicted you is nothing; do not let it disturb your face, your heart; do not fear this sickness or any other sickness, nor any sharp or hurtful thing. Am I not here, I who have the honor to be your mother? Are you not in my shadow and under my protection? Am I not the source of your joy? Are you not in the hollow of my mantle, in the crossing of my arms? Do you need anything more? (*Nican Mopohua*, nos. 118-119)

Having received Our Lady's assurance, Saint Juan Diego carried out his mission immediately by returning once more to the Bishop, explaining to him the desire of the ever Virgin Mary for the building of a sacred little house and bringing to the Bishop the sign of the truth of Our Lady's message for him.

We, too, receive Our Lady's assurance in those same encouraging words: What afflicts you is nothing; do not let it disturb you; do not fear; she is here; she is your mother; she protects you; she is the source of your joy; she is holding you in her arms.

NOVENA PRAYER *to* Our Lady *of* Guadalupe

O Virgin Mother of God, we fly to your protection and beg your intercession against the darkness and sin which ever more envelop the world and menace the Church. Your Son, Our Lord Jesus Christ, gave you to us as our mother as He died on the Cross for our salvation. So, too, in 1531, when darkness and sin beset us, He sent you, as Our Lady of Guadalupe, on Tepeyac to lead us to Him Who alone is our light and our salvation.

Through your apparitions on Tepeyac and your abiding presence with us on the miraculous mantle of your messenger, Saint Juan Diego, millions of souls converted to faith in your Divine Son. Through this novena and our consecration to you, we humbly implore your intercession for our daily conversion of life to Him and the conversion of millions more who do not yet believe in Him. In our homes and in our nation, lead us to Him Who alone wins the victory over sin and darkness in us and in the world.

Unite our hearts to your Immaculate Heart so that they may find their true and lasting home in the Most Sacred Heart of Jesus. Ever guide us along the pilgrimage of life to our eternal home with Him. So may our hearts, one with yours, always trust in God's promise of salvation, in His never-failing mercy toward all who turn to Him with a humble and contrite heart. Through this novena and our consecration to you, O Virgin of Guadalupe, lead all souls in America and throughout the world to your Divine Son in Whose name we pray. Amen.

DAY FIVE

Yesterday, our reflection focused on the trust that Saint Juan Diego placed in Our Lady of Guadalupe, even when difficult circumstances in his life tempted him to avoid a personal encounter with her, which she corrected with the love and mercy of a mother redirecting the faltering footsteps of her child.

Now, let us turn our attention to the last direction of the Virgin Mother of God, Our Lady of Guadalupe, which is that we are to become her messengers, just as she called Saint Juan Diego to be her messenger to Bishop Juan de Zumárraga. Juan Diego experienced numerous temptations from Satan to avoid Our Lady's mission. An early snare tempted him to excuse himself from the mission because he was the wrong person to carry it out, describing himself as "just a man from the country" and because he was not someone to approach the Bishop, declaring that the Bishop's residence "is not my place to go or to stay" (*Nican Mopohua*, no. 55).

All of us can easily give way to doubt and fear before the challenge of living in Christ in our totally secularized culture. There is the tendency to doubt God's grace and to give way to fear in responding to its "costly" demands. There is the temptation to think that we must devise some program, "some magic formula" (Pope Saint John Paul II, *Novo Millennio Ineunte*), to transform the world. Yet it is Christ, alive for us in the Church, Who alone shows us the way. It is our humble and confident following of Christ which will transform us and our world. To help us follow

Him, Our Lord, as He was dying upon the cross, gave us His Mother as our Mother.

By the mystery of the Divine Maternity, the Immaculate Heart of the Blessed Virgin Mary, assumed into glory, never ceases to beat with love for us, the children whom her Divine Son gave to her, as He was dying upon the Cross. When Our Lord pronounced the words, "Woman, behold thy son" (Jn 19, 26) to His Mother and "Behold thy mother" (Jn 19, 27) to Saint John the Apostle and Evangelist, standing at the foot of the cross, He expressed an essential reality of the salvation He was winning for us: the full cooperation of His Mother, the Blessed Virgin Mary, in His saving work. The Mother of God the Son Incarnate is the Mother of Divine Grace at work in our souls.

The work that the Virgin of Guadalupe gave to Saint Juan Diego is the work that Our Lord asks us to continue today: It is the work of evangelization in the Church and in the world. Her humbling words to Saint Juan Diego are her words to us, too: "I have no lack of servants, of messengers, to whom I can give the task" (*Nican Mopohua*, no. 58). The Queen of Heaven can choose anyone to accomplish her desire, but she, Our Blessed Mother, has chosen you and me, her children, to be her messengers, to carry the Word of God, her Divine Son, into the hearts of all, so that they may unite their heart to her Immaculate Heart, through whom our hearts become more intimately united to the Sacred Heart of Jesus. Accordingly, let her words to Saint Juan Diego fill us with virtuous courage as we persevere in this novena. "I, personally, the ever Virgin Holy Mary, I, who am the Mother of God, sent you as my messenger" (*Nican Mopohua*, no. 62).

NOVENA PRAYER
to Our Lady *of* Guadalupe

O Virgin Mother of God, we fly to your protection and beg your intercession against the darkness and sin which ever more envelop the world and menace the Church. Your Son, Our Lord Jesus Christ, gave you to us as our mother as He died on the Cross for our salvation. So, too, in 1531, when darkness and sin beset us, He sent you, as Our Lady of Guadalupe, on Tepeyac to lead us to Him Who alone is our light and our salvation.

Through your apparitions on Tepeyac and your abiding presence with us on the miraculous mantle of your messenger, Saint Juan Diego, millions of souls converted to faith in your Divine Son. Through this novena and our consecration to you, we humbly implore your intercession for our daily conversion of life to Him and the conversion of millions more who do not yet believe in Him. In our homes and in our nation, lead us to Him Who alone wins the victory over sin and darkness in us and in the world.

Unite our hearts to your Immaculate Heart so that they may find their true and lasting home in the Most Sacred Heart of Jesus. Ever guide us along the pilgrimage of life to our eternal home with Him. So may our hearts, one with yours, always trust in God's promise of salvation, in His never-failing mercy toward all who turn to Him with a humble and contrite heart. Through this novena and our consecration to you, O Virgin of Guadalupe, lead all souls in America and throughout the world to your Divine Son in Whose name we pray. Amen.

DAY SIX

In the economy of salvation, the Blessed Virgin Mary, crowned at her Assumption as Queen of Heaven and Earth, is the Mediatrix of All Grace. She, the first and best disciple of her Divine Son, cooperates fully in His Redemptive work from the moment of His conception to the moment of His death on the cross, when her Immaculate Heart was mystically pierced at the piercing of His Sacred Heart by the Roman soldier's spear. Always one in her glorious Immaculate Heart with His Most Sacred Heart, she continues, with maternal love, to be the channel of the immeasurable and unceasing graces that pour forth from His glorious-pierced Heart into the hearts of all the faithful. She is the Mother of Divine Grace.

Our Lady's work as Mediatrix became manifest with the establishment of a "sacred little house," a place of pilgrimage, in Tepeyac in 1531, whence she might show the mercy of God to all her children of America and of the world. As the great sign of her maternal desire to make us one with her Divine Son and, therefore, recipients of the immeasurable outpouring of God's mercy, God miraculously left her image on the tilma or mantle of Saint Juan Diego. To this day, the Sacred Image, which has no human explanation as to its origin and whose fabric, cactus cloth, should have disintegrated some thirty to forty years after her apparitions, remains intact and radiates a miraculous maternal love.

Within eight years from the date of Our Lady's apparitions at Guadalupe, nearly nine million Native Americans converted to the Catholic faith, giving up the diabolical practice of human sacrifice and embracing the Christian way of life with remarkable fervor and fidelity. What is more, the European explorers and settlers, and the Native Americans, who were on the verge of a most bloody conflict, united to form a new culture, the mestiza culture, which yet today looks to the Virgin of Guadalupe as its source and inspiration.

I have personally experienced her maternal love while gazing upon the tilma. Through her maternal love, Our Lady of Guadalupe brings her children to her Divine Son, the only Savior of the world, in Whom we discover the wonder of our daily life, for God indeed dwells with us in the Church and within our souls.

When we come to her Shrine, Our Lady of Guadalupe, with deepest maternal affection, manifests to us the great mystery of God's love for us, inviting us to have complete confidence in His promises. Making our consecration to her, she draws us to encounter her Divine Son, the fulfillment of all God the Father's promises. She draws us especially to the Sacraments of Penance and of the Most Holy Eucharist, so that we may know directly in our lives the fulfillment of God's promise of liberation from sin and death, His promise of eternal salvation. Making our consecration at the Shrine of Our Lady of Guadalupe is our response to her pure and perfect love by totally giving our hearts to her Immaculate Heart, through whom we are ever more perfectly united to the glorious-pierced Heart of her Divine Son, Jesus Savior.

NOVENA PRAYER *to* Our Lady *of* Guadalupe

O Virgin Mother of God, we fly to your protection and beg your intercession against the darkness and sin which ever more envelop the world and menace the Church. Your Son, Our Lord Jesus Christ, gave you to us as our mother as He died on the Cross for our salvation. So, too, in 1531, when darkness and sin beset us, He sent you, as Our Lady of Guadalupe, on Tepeyac to lead us to Him Who alone is our light and our salvation.

Through your apparitions on Tepeyac and your abiding presence with us on the miraculous mantle of your messenger, Saint Juan Diego, millions of souls converted to faith in your Divine Son. Through this novena and our consecration to you, we humbly implore your intercession for our daily conversion of life to Him and the conversion of millions more who do not yet believe in Him. In our homes and in our nation, lead us to Him Who alone wins the victory over sin and darkness in us and in the world.

Unite our hearts to your Immaculate Heart so that they may find their true and lasting home in the Most Sacred Heart of Jesus. Ever guide us along the pilgrimage of life to our eternal home with Him. So may our hearts, one with yours, always trust in God's promise of salvation, in His never-failing mercy toward all who turn to Him with a humble and contrite heart. Through this novena and our consecration to you, O Virgin of Guadalupe, lead all souls in America and throughout the world to your Divine Son in Whose name we pray. Amen.

DAY SEVEN

When Our Lady provided Saint Juan Diego with the sign which the Bishop requested, she insisted on the importance of the chapel as the locus of the manifestation of God's all-merciful love:

> My youngest son, these different kinds of flowers are the proof, the sign that you will take to the Bishop; you will tell him from me that in them he is to see my wish and that therefore he is to carry out my wish, my will; and you, you who are my messenger, in you I place my absolute trust. And I strictly order you that only alone, in the Bishop's presence, will you open your tilma and show him what you are carrying; and you will tell him everything exactly, you will tell him that I ordered you to climb to the top of the little hill to cut the flowers, and everything you saw and admired; so that you can convince the Governing Priest, so that he will then do what is entrusted to him, to build my little sacred house that I have asked for (*Nican Mopohua*, nos. 137-142).

In fact, from the time of the apparitions of Our Lady of Guadalupe and the enshrinement of her miraculous image in the succession of chapels and churches built near Tepeyac

Hill, the devotion to Our Lady has favored a profound and rich life of prayer and divine worship.

In the end, everything regarding the apparitions is directed to the establishment of the chapel as a place of pilgrimage, of a privileged encounter with the Lord through the mediation of His Virgin Mother.

The presentation of the sign to Bishop Juan de Zumárraga is remarkable.

> And then he opened his white tilma, in the hollow of which were the flowers. And all the different flowers, like those from Castille, fell to the floor. Then and there his tilma became the sign, there suddenly appeared the Beloved Image of the Perfect Virgin Saint Mary, Mother of God, in the form and figure in which it is now, where it is preserved in her beloved little house, in her sacred little house in Tepeyac, which is called Guadalupe …
>
> And the Bishop got up, and untied Juan Diego's garment, his tilma, from his neck where it was tied, on which appeared the venerable sign of the Heavenly Queen. And then he took it and placed it in his private chapel. And Juan Diego still stayed for the day in the Bishop's house, who still kept him there. And on the next day he [the Bishop] said to him: "Come, let's go so you can show me where it is that the venerable will of the Queen of Heaven wants Her chapel built" (*Nican Mopohua*, nos. 181-184, and 188-192).

If we are to be messengers of Our Lady, our hearts must be in union with her Immaculate Heart. Let us, therefore, build a "sacred little house" to Our Lady of Guadalupe in our hearts, setting a spiritual tilma in a place wherefrom, under the interior contemplation of her maternal gaze, she can prepare our hearts to make a pilgrimage to a holy place, where we can truly encounter her Divine Son, Jesus Christ, come to know Him more fully and to love Him more ardently, especially in the Sacraments of Penance and the Holy Eucharist.

I invite you on such a pilgrimage. At the Church of the Shrine of Our Lady of Guadalupe in La Crosse, Wisconsin, I encourage you to make the Solemn Act of Consecration to Our Lady of Guadalupe. The Shrine is a Vatican-approved place of pilgrimage, affiliated with the Basilica of Saint Mary Major in Rome and with the Basilica of Our Lady of Guadalupe in Mexico City. This affiliation means that those who come to the Shrine on pilgrimage receives the same graces and blessings as if they had gone on pilgrimage to the Basilica of Saint Mary Major or the Basilica of Our Lady of Guadalupe.

NOVENA PRAYER *to* Our Lady *of* Guadalupe

O Virgin Mother of God, we fly to your protection and beg your intercession against the darkness and sin which ever more envelop the world and menace the Church. Your Son, Our Lord Jesus Christ, gave you to us as our mother as He died on the Cross for our salvation. So, too, in 1531, when darkness and sin beset us, He sent you, as Our Lady of Guadalupe, on Tepeyac to lead us to Him Who alone is our light and our salvation.

Through your apparitions on Tepeyac and your abiding presence with us on the miraculous mantle of your messenger, Saint Juan Diego, millions of souls converted to faith in your Divine Son. Through this novena and our consecration to you, we humbly implore your intercession for our daily conversion of life to Him and the conversion of millions more who do not yet believe in Him. In our homes and in our nation, lead us to Him Who alone wins the victory over sin and darkness in us and in the world.

Unite our hearts to your Immaculate Heart so that they may find their true and lasting home in the Most Sacred Heart of Jesus. Ever guide us along the pilgrimage of life to our eternal home with Him. So may our hearts, one with yours, always trust in God's promise of salvation, in His never-failing mercy toward all who turn to Him with a humble and contrite heart. Through this novena and our consecration to you, O Virgin of Guadalupe, lead all souls in America and throughout the world to your Divine Son in Whose name we pray. Amen.

DAY EIGHT

In what context does the Virgin of Guadalupe propose to teach us the mystery of God's ever faithful and all-merciful love? It is in the context of our entrance into the House of God to pray and to offer to Him the worship which He Himself inspires in us and strengthens us to carry out. "I want very much that they build my sacred little house here," Our Lady instructed the Church in Mexico through her messenger Saint Juan Diego. Her intention for the "sacred little house," the church, is to "show" her Divine Son, Jesus Christ, "exalt Him upon making Him manifest," and "give Him to all people" in her maternal love through prayer, devotion, and the Sacred Liturgy, especially the Sacraments of the Church (Cf. *Nican Mopohua*, no. 26-28).

In the Sacred Liturgy, Christ Himself acts in our midst for the glory of God and for our eternal salvation. In fact, it is only in the House of God that our greatest hunger and thirst are satisfied. In His dwelling with us through the Church, we know God in the forgiveness of our sins through the Sacrament of Penance and in the incomparable gift of the Body, Blood, Soul, and Divinity of Christ, the fruit of the Eucharistic Sacrifice given as Heavenly Bread to us in Holy Communion. Our Lady requests the building of a chapel or church because the Church's doctrine and discipline are the irreplaceable conditions for the encounter with Christ and the daily conversion of life to Christ by following Him on the only way which leads to eternal life, the way of the Cross (Cf. Mt 16, 24).

Mary, our Mother, preserved from all stain of Original Sin, understands better than any of us the wiles of Satan and the profound harm and eternal death itself, which come to us through sin. She witnessed the effects of the sin of our First Parents and of our actual sins in the Passion and Death of her Divine Son. She, therefore, stands ever ready to point out to us Satan's allurements and deceptions, and to sustain us in times of great trial and temptation by leading us to her Son alive for us in the Church, especially through the Sacraments of Penance and the Holy Eucharist. By drawing close to the Immaculate Heart of Our Blessed Mother, under the title of Our Lady of Guadalupe, we come to understand ever better the effects of sin in our lives and upon our world; we come to understand our need to go to her Son for the grace of conversion of life and the transformation of our world. In her maternal love, she leads us in the way of the humility which Our Lord teaches us in the Gospel, so that we give our hearts totally to Him, with confident trust in His never-failing and all-merciful love (Cf. Lk 9, 48).

The Shrine of Our Lady of Guadalupe in La Crosse, Wisconsin, was built to further the mission of Our Lady of Guadalupe, so that many more might know her maternal love and, through her love, know their Savior. In the planning and construction of the Church, every effort was made to reflect the ineffable beauty of God and of His faithful and enduring love of us, most especially in the Redemptive Incarnation of His only-begotten Son.

I invite you to come to the Shrine of Our Lady of Guadalupe on a pilgrimage to make your Official Act of Consecration to her as the culmination of the Nine-Month Novena. Please tell others to come, too. Let them know that the Shrine is a Vatican-approved place of pilgrimage, affiliated with the Basilica of Saint Mary Major in Rome and the Basilica of Our Lady of Guadalupe in Mexico City. Let everyone know that those who come on pilgrimage to the Shrine receives the same graces and blessings as if they had gone on pilgrimage to those two great Basilicas.

NOVENA PRAYER *to* Our Lady *of* Guadalupe

O Virgin Mother of God, we fly to your protection and beg your intercession against the darkness and sin which ever more envelop the world and menace the Church. Your Son, Our Lord Jesus Christ, gave you to us as our mother as He died on the Cross for our salvation. So, too, in 1531, when darkness and sin beset us, He sent you, as Our Lady of Guadalupe, on Tepeyac to lead us to Him Who alone is our light and our salvation.

Through your apparitions on Tepeyac and your abiding presence with us on the miraculous mantle of your messenger, Saint Juan Diego, millions of souls converted to faith in your Divine Son. Through this novena and our consecration to you, we humbly implore your intercession for our daily conversion of life to Him and the conversion of millions more who do not yet believe in Him. In our homes and in our nation, lead us to Him Who alone wins the victory over sin and darkness in us and in the world.

Unite our hearts to your Immaculate Heart so that they may find their true and lasting home in the Most Sacred Heart of Jesus. Ever guide us along the pilgrimage of life to our eternal home with Him. So may our hearts, one with yours, always trust in God's promise of salvation, in His never-failing mercy toward all who turn to Him with a humble and contrite heart. Through this novena and our consecration to you, O Virgin of Guadalupe, lead all souls in America and throughout the world to your Divine Son in Whose name we pray. Amen.

DAY NINE

At the Shrine of Our Lady of Guadalupe, we celebrate the mystery of God's dwelling with us in His only-begotten Son, conceived in the womb of the Blessed Virgin Mary, which the Virgin proclaimed from the moment of her first apparition to Saint Juan Diego on December 9th of 1531. It is the same mystery of God's immeasurable mercy and love toward us that Our Lady of Guadalupe announced in each of her apparitions over the three days which followed. It is the mystery which she never ceases to announce through her miraculous image which the hand of God Himself left for us on the mantle (tilma) of Saint Juan Diego on December 12th, the day of her final apparition. On that wonderful day, the Virgin provided to Bishop Juan de Zumárraga the sign of the truth of her apparitions, which he had requested from Saint Juan Diego: the miraculous flowering of roses in the middle of winter on a barren and stony hilltop. But, even more wonderfully, God provided the ultimate sign of that truth: He imprinted the image of the Virgin of Guadalupe on the mantle of Saint Juan Diego, so that, in a certain and true sense, she could continue to appear to His children who would come on pilgrimage to meet her and, in meeting her, to meet her Divine Son, above all in the Sacraments of Penance and the Most Holy Eucharist.

Coming to the Shrine on pilgrimage, the pilgrim leaves familiar surroundings to climb the Pilgrim Way leading to the Shrine Church out of a desire for a personal encounter with Our Lady, who draws us into an even more personal encounter with her Divine Son, Jesus Christ. The Virgin of Guadalupe brings us to meet her Divine Son in the Sacraments of Penance and the Holy Eucharist. The pilgrim indeed sees Our Lord, and encounters Our Lord, while praying in the Shrine Church before the Blessed Sacrament reposed in the tabernacle, in the Sacrament of Penance and, most wonderfully of all, through participation in the Eucharistic Sacrifice and in the reception of the incomparable fruit of that Sacrifice, the Body of Christ as the Heavenly Bread of our earthly pilgrimage.

The true pilgrim comes to the holy place with the deep desire for that personal encounter with Christ, to know Christ more and, therefore, to desire to encounter Him worthily in the Sacraments. The more pilgrims meet Christ in the Sacraments, the more they will want to love Him and to serve Him by bringing His love to their brothers and sisters, especially those who are in most need. Coming on pilgrimage to Our Lady of Guadalupe, so that she may lead us to her Son, Our Lord, we understand that communion with Him in sacred worship finds its ultimate expression in the truth and love according to which we conduct our daily lives. True worship of God inspires and strengthens us to do the will of God in all things. Ultimately, the pilgrimage attains its end when Christ has come to dwell in the heart of each pilgrim, in the pilgrim's home, through the mystery of His living presence with us in the Church.

I encourage you to make a pilgrimage to the Shrine of Our Lady of Guadalupe in La Crosse, Wisconsin, in order to make your Act of Consecration to Our Lady of Guadalupe. However, if such a pilgrimage is not possible, please make your Act of Consecration at your parish church, before the Blessed Sacrament reposed in the tabernacle.

NOVENA PRAYER *to* Our Lady *of* Guadalupe

O Virgin Mother of God, we fly to your protection and beg your intercession against the darkness and sin which ever more envelop the world and menace the Church. Your Son, Our Lord Jesus Christ, gave you to us as our mother as He died on the Cross for our salvation. So, too, in 1531, when darkness and sin beset us, He sent you, as Our Lady of Guadalupe, on Tepeyac to lead us to Him Who alone is our light and our salvation.

Through your apparitions on Tepeyac and your abiding presence with us on the miraculous mantle of your messenger, Saint Juan Diego, millions of souls converted to faith in your Divine Son. Through this novena and our consecration to you, we humbly implore your intercession for our daily conversion of life to Him and the conversion of millions more who do not yet believe in Him. In our homes and in our nation, lead us to Him Who alone wins the victory over sin and darkness in us and in the world.

Unite our hearts to your Immaculate Heart so that they may find their true and lasting home in the Most Sacred Heart of Jesus. Ever guide us along the pilgrimage of life to our eternal home with Him. So may our hearts, one with yours, always trust in God's promise of salvation, in His never-failing mercy toward all who turn to Him with a humble and contrite heart. Through this novena and our consecration to you, O Virgin of Guadalupe, lead all souls in America and throughout the world to your Divine Son in Whose name we pray. Amen.

ACT OF CONSECRATION *to* Our Lady *of* Guadalupe

DECEMBER 12

O Holy Virgin Mary, Mother of God and my compassionate Mother,[1] I, with Saint Juan Diego, your faithful and courageous messenger, prostrate myself before your Beloved Image.[2] With all my heart, I, too, desire to be your messenger. With Saint Juan Diego, may my heart be totally one with your Sorrowful and Immaculate Heart, perfectly united to the glorious-pierced Heart of your Divine Son, Our Lord and Savior Jesus Christ.

Conscious of my sins, of the evils oppressing the world and threatening the Church, and of the unrelenting guile of Satan, "the father of lies,"[3] I come before you, seeking your protection and invoking your intercession, that I may belong totally to your Divine Son, King of the Universe and King of my heart. Incarnate in your womb at Nazareth and born of you at Bethlehem, He came into the world to save me from sin and everlasting death. Obtaining my eternal salvation by His death on the Cross, He gave you to me to be my mother forever.[4] As His Mother, bring Him to me, and, as my Mother, bring me to Him Who alone is "the way, the truth, and the life,"[5] teaching me, as you taught the wine stewards at the Wedding Feast of Cana: "Do whatever He tells you."[6]

Before the troubles, the miseries, and the pains which afflict me, the world, and the Church,[7] I am tempted to give way to discouragement and to claim helplessness.[8] In moments of temptation, remind me that you have chosen me to be your messenger and that Our Lord, without measure and without cease, sustains with the sevenfold grace of the Holy Spirit a humble and contrite heart.[9] Help me to remain, with you, one in heart with the Sacred Heart of Jesus, trusting that God's promises to me will indeed be fulfilled.[10] Keeping me "in the hollow of your mantle" and "in the crossing of your arms,"[11] let no trouble, no misery, no pain obscure or diminish my service as your faithful messenger. Rather, with maternal love, encourage and strengthen me to take up steadfastly and joyfully the cross of pure and selfless love, which is indeed my only hope, my only way to joy and peace here and now, and to its fullness in the eternal life of Heaven.[12]

Under your protection and through your intercession, may I, every day and at every moment of the day, give myself anew to Jesus, "my Lord and my God,"[13] and may I, with you, draw to Him the many who do not yet know Him and the many who have known Him but are now far away from Him. Please intercede for me, that, through my conversion of life to Him and through His grace at work in my heart, my every thought, attitude, word, and action may attract others to Him Who alone is their salvation. Please intercede for my family and my homeland, that Christ the King may rule in all hearts from His Most Sacred Heart, pierced by the soldier's spear as He died on Calvary and now seated in eternal glory at the right hand of the Father, dispelling all darkness, all sin, and all attraction to sin.

O Virgin Mother of God and my compassionate Mother, prostrate before your Beloved Image, I now unite my heart forever to your Sorrowful and Immaculate Heart, finding my true and lasting home in the Most Sacred Heart of

Jesus. I consecrate myself to you, the Perfect Virgin, Saint Mary of Guadalupe.[14] I promise to be your ever faithful and courageous messenger on earth. Thus, at the end of my earthly pilgrimage, may I be forever in your company, together with the angels and all the saints, praising and glorifying God – Father, Son, and Holy Spirit. Please accept my Act of Consecration and never let me betray the gift of myself to you which, today, I make with all my heart. Amen.

---

[1] *Nican Mopohua*, nos. 26 and 29.

[2] *Nican Mopohua*, no.183.

[3] Jn 8, 44.

[4] Cf. Jn 19, 26-27.

[5] Jn 14, 6.

[6] Jn 2, 5.

[7] Cf. *Nican Mopohua*, no. 32.

[8] Cf. *Nican Mopohua*, nos. 54-56 and 111-116.

[9] Cf. Is 57, 15.

[10] Cf. Lk 2, 45.

[11] *Nican Mopohua*, no. 119.

[12] Cf. Mt 10, 38; 16, 34; Mk 8, 34; Lk 9, 23; Jn 12, 25-26.

[13] Jn 20, 28.

[14] *Nican Mopohua*, no. 208.

DAILY PRAYER *of* THOSE CONSECRATED *to* Our Lady *of* Guadalupe

Prayed from December 13th every day until December 2nd of the following year.

O Virgin Mother of God, Our Lady of Guadalupe, at the beginning of a new day, I renew my consecration to you, my compassionate mother. I pray that, today, I, with Saint Juan Diego, may be your ever faithful messenger.

Please intercede for the conversion of my heart to Christ, your Divine Son. Throughout this day, may my heart, one with your Sorrowful and Immaculate Heart, rest ever more perfectly in His glorious-pierced Heart. In all things, may I do what He is asking of me. In difficulties, trials, and temptations, may I, in the embrace of your arms, trust His promise to win in me the victory over sin and death.

I pray also for the many who have abandoned Christ and for the many who do not yet know Him. May you bring millions of souls to Christ, and may I, your messenger, draw souls to Him Who alone is our salvation.

O Lady of Guadalupe, I place within your mantle my family and my homeland, asking that Christ may reign in all hearts from His Most Sacred Heart. At your pleading, may He pour forth into humble and contrite hearts the sevenfold gift of the Holy Spirit dispelling from them all darkness and sin, and inflaming them with divine truth and love.

May I, alive in Christ, advance today on the earthly pilgrimage to my lasting home with you and with the angels and all the saints, where we shall forever praise and glorify God – Father, Son, and Holy Spirit. With all my heart, I ask this in Christ, your Divine Son, my Lord and my Savior. Amen.

NINE MONTH NOVENA
to Our Lady *of* Guadalupe

MARCH ☙ REFLECTION ONE

Today, we begin our Nine-Month Novena to Our Lady of Guadalupe.

Our Lady of Guadalupe first appeared to Saint Juan Diego just before dawn on a Saturday morning, December 9, 1531. Although the home of Juan Diego was in Cuauhtitlán, his spiritual home was Tlatelolco, the place of his baptism and of his ongoing instruction in the Catholic faith. Our Lady favored with her apparition and chose as her messenger a humble Christian who was seeking to deepen his knowledge of the faith through instruction from the priest whom he identifies as an image of Christ alive for us in the Church.

When Our Lady began to speak with him, she immediately declared the truth of her being, of her relationship with God as Mother of God the Son Incarnate, and of her relationship with Juan Diego, as with all Christians. She declared:

> Know, know for sure my dearest and youngest son, that I am truly the ever perfect Holy Virgin Mary, who has the honor to be Mother of the one true God for whom we all live, the Creator of people, the Lord of all around us and of what is close to us, the Lord of Heaven, the Lord of Earth (*Nican Mopohua*, no. 26).

What is primary for Our Lady in her relationship with Juan Diego and in his collaboration as her messenger is the truth that she is the Virgin Mother of God the Son Incarnate Who is the King of Heaven and Earth and Who alone is our salvation.

The first lesson which Our Lady of Guadalupe teaches us to equip us for today's grave crisis is the inseparable unity of truth and love. We cannot truly love another person while also disregarding or betraying the truth which should inform every relationship. The fundamental approach to the crisis of the family, of society, and of the Church is the knowledge of truth and the practice of it with love.

NOVENA PRAYER
to Our Lady *of* Guadalupe

O Virgin Mother of God, we fly to your protection and beg your intercession against the darkness and sin which ever more envelop the world and menace the Church. Your Son, Our Lord Jesus Christ, gave you to us as our mother as He died on the Cross for our salvation. So, too, in 1531, when darkness and sin beset us, He sent you, as Our Lady of Guadalupe, on Tepeyac to lead us to Him Who alone is our light and our salvation.

Through your apparitions on Tepeyac and your abiding presence with us on the miraculous mantle of your messenger, Saint Juan Diego, millions of souls converted to faith in your Divine Son. Through this novena and our consecration to you, we humbly implore your intercession for our daily conversion of life to Him and the conversion of millions more who do not yet believe in Him. In our homes and in our nation, lead us to Him Who alone wins the victory over sin and darkness in us and in the world.

Unite our hearts to your Immaculate Heart so that they may find their true and lasting home in the Most Sacred Heart of Jesus. Ever guide us along the pilgrimage of life to our eternal home with Him. So may our hearts, one with yours, always trust in God's promise of salvation, in His never-failing mercy toward all who turn to Him with a humble and contrite heart. Through this novena and our consecration to you, O Virgin of Guadalupe, lead all souls in America and throughout the world to your Divine Son in Whose name we pray. Amen.

MARCH ☙ REFLECTION TWO

This month marks the beginning of our Nine-Month Novena to Our Lady of Guadalupe, culminating in our Consecration to her on December 12th of this year.

Why, some may ask, make a Novena and Consecration to Our Lady of Guadalupe? What help does the Mother of God bring to our world in these tumultuous times? What help did she bring at Tepeyac in 1531?

Our Lady brings her Divine Son, Christ the Lord Who alone is the salvation of the world. After identifying herself to Saint Juan Diego as the Mother of God, Our Lady declared her mission:

> I want very much that they build my sacred little house here, in which I will show Him, I will exalt Him upon making Him manifest, I will give Him to all people in all my personal love, Him that is my compassionate gaze, Him that is my help, Him that is my salvation (*Nican Mopohua*, nos. 26-28).

This mission for Saint Juan Diego's time and place is just as much for ours today. Her mission, which is in total union with the saving mission of her Divine Son, is ongoing, until the Last Day. Our Lady does not propose some idea or some political action to address the various crises confronting us. No, she proposes a person, the person of her Divine Son. She proposes the most intimate union of heart with Him, with His Most Sacred Heart, as the only way to obtain mercy and ultimately eternal life. She tells Juan Diego that Christ is in fact her "compassionate gaze," even as He is her "help," her "salvation."

In this way, too, she shows us what is the help which we offer to the world and the Church in a time of great turmoil. We offer Jesus Christ. As much as is possible, we desire that those who look upon us will see the face of Christ and be drawn to Him Who alone can save them.

NOVENA PRAYER
to Our Lady *of* Guadalupe

O Virgin Mother of God, we fly to your protection and beg your intercession against the darkness and sin which ever more envelop the world and menace the Church. Your Son, Our Lord Jesus Christ, gave you to us as our mother as He died on the Cross for our salvation. So, too, in 1531, when darkness and sin beset us, He sent you, as Our Lady of Guadalupe, on Tepeyac to lead us to Him Who alone is our light and our salvation.

Through your apparitions on Tepeyac and your abiding presence with us on the miraculous mantle of your messenger, Saint Juan Diego, millions of souls converted to faith in your Divine Son. Through this novena and our consecration to you, we humbly implore your intercession for our daily conversion of life to Him and the conversion of millions more who do not yet believe in Him. In our homes and in our nation, lead us to Him Who alone wins the victory over sin and darkness in us and in the world.

Unite our hearts to your Immaculate Heart so that they may find their true and lasting home in the Most Sacred Heart of Jesus. Ever guide us along the pilgrimage of life to our eternal home with Him. So may our hearts, one with yours, always trust in God's promise of salvation, in His never-failing mercy toward all who turn to Him with a humble and contrite heart. Through this novena and our consecration to you, O Virgin of Guadalupe, lead all souls in America and throughout the world to your Divine Son in Whose name we pray. Amen.

APRIL ∽ REFLECTION ONE

As our first month of the Nine-Month Novena concludes and our second month begins, some of us may be experiencing the worst temptations from Satan to surrender and stop praying the Novena Prayer every day.

Throughout the days of the apparitions, Saint Juan Diego was subject to the temptations of Satan, who placed in him the doubt that he was worthy and capable of carrying out the directions and orders of the Heavenly Queen. After his first visit to the Bishop, he was convinced that only someone of higher social status could carry out Our Lady's mission. In a rather eloquent way, he described his own lowliness to the Virgin Mother of God:

> So I beg you, my Lady, my Queen, my little Girl, to have one of the nobles who are held in esteem, one who is known, respected, honored, have him carry on, take your venerable breath, your venerable word, so that he will be believed. Because I am really just a man from the country, I'm the porter's rope, I'm a back frame, just a tail, a wing; I myself need to be led, carried on someone's back; there, where you sent me, it is not my place to go or to stay, my little Girl, my littlest Daughter, my Lady, my Girl. Please, excuse me, I will afflict your face, your heart; I will fall into your anger, your displeasure, my Lady Mistress (*Nican Mopohua*, nos. 54-56).

But the Mother of God, the Mother of Divine Grace, responded by confirming him as her messenger, assuring him that he, too, was called to carry out the mission of bringing God Incarnate to the world, to his brothers and sisters.

Our Lady of Guadalupe assured him that she has many upon whom to call for the mission of her messenger, but that Juan Diego has been called and, therefore, must trust that he can carry out the mission. She replies to him:

> Listen my youngest son, know for sure that I have no lack of servants, of messengers, to whom I can give the task of carrying my breath, my word, so that they carry out my will; but it is necessary that you, personally, go and plead, that by your intercession, my wish, my will, become a reality. And I beg you, my youngest son, and I strictly order you, to go again tomorrow to see the Bishop. And in my name, make him know, make him hear my wish, my will, so that he will bring into being, he will build, my sacred house that I ask of him. And carefully tell him again how I, personally, the ever Virgin Holy Mary, I, who am the Mother of God, sent you as my messenger (*Nican Mopohua*, nos. 58-62).

In the battle for the truth, we must never give way to discouragement which is always the first temptation of the devil. When we are tempted to be discouraged or to be defeated, let us recall the vision of the final victory of Christ's Redemptive Incarnation, recounted in the Book of Revelation. In the vision, Satan is determined to destroy the "woman clothed with the sun" (Rv 12, 1) and her Son. But the Divine Son of Mary is "caught up to God and to his throne" (Rv 12, 5). Thus, He brings his victory over sin and death to its fullness. In fact, the image of the Virgin of Guadalupe which God left for us on the tilma (mantle) of Saint Juan Diego is the "woman clothed with the sun" who carries in her womb the Savior of the world.

Our Lady's motherly words to Saint Juan Diego speak to us, too, as they reflect a fundamental truth of the faith: Christ's dwelling with us in His holy Church, the Indwelling of the Holy Spirit in our souls, enables even the weakest person to carry out God's will with heroic virtue. Only with the aid of God's grace, through the intercession of Our Lady, Mediatrix of All Graces, will we persevere in this Novena and Consecration.

NOVENA PRAYER *to* Our Lady *of* Guadalupe

O Virgin Mother of God, we fly to your protection and beg your intercession against the darkness and sin which ever more envelop the world and menace the Church. Your Son, Our Lord Jesus Christ, gave you to us as our mother as He died on the Cross for our salvation. So, too, in 1531, when darkness and sin beset us, He sent you, as Our Lady of Guadalupe, on Tepeyac to lead us to Him Who alone is our light and our salvation.

Through your apparitions on Tepeyac and your abiding presence with us on the miraculous mantle of your messenger, Saint Juan Diego, millions of souls converted to faith in your Divine Son. Through this novena and our consecration to you, we humbly implore your intercession for our daily conversion of life to Him and the conversion of millions more who do not yet believe in Him. In our homes and in our nation, lead us to Him Who alone wins the victory over sin and darkness in us and in the world.

Unite our hearts to your Immaculate Heart so that they may find their true and lasting home in the Most Sacred Heart of Jesus. Ever guide us along the pilgrimage of life to our eternal home with Him. So may our hearts, one with yours, always trust in God's promise of salvation, in His never-failing mercy toward all who turn to Him with a humble and contrite heart. Through this novena and our consecration to you, O Virgin of Guadalupe, lead all souls in America and throughout the world to your Divine Son in Whose name we pray. Amen.

APRIL ও REFLECTION TWO

Making the Nine-Month Novena to the Blessed Virgin Mary under her title of Our Lady of Guadalupe, entrusting ourselves to her guidance and protection and confiding to her intercession our many intentions for the Church and for the world, we rejoice in the perfect union of her Immaculate Heart with the Most Sacred Heart of her Divine Son, Our Lord and Savior. As the Virgin Mother of God was totally for Christ from the very first moment of her conception, so we, following her example and seeking her intercession, desire to be more and more totally for Christ. We rejoice in the fulfillment of the prophecy of Isaiah regarding the Virginal Conception and Birth of the Savior: "Therefore the Lord himself will give you a sign. Behold, a virgin shall conceive and bear a son, and shall call his name Emmanuel" (Isaiah 7, 14).

These words attained their fulfillment at the Annunciation. The Virgin Mary, with her "*Fiat mihi secundum verbum tuum*" ("Let it be done to me according to your word," [Lk 1, 38]), became the Mother of God, the Theotokos, "God-Bearer" to the world. She exercised her mission of God-Bearer, in a most extraordinary way, on Tepeyac Hill from December 9th to 12th of 1531 by means of her apparitions to Saint Juan Diego and his uncle Juan Bernardino. Her exercise of the mission continues to our day through the miraculous imprint of her image on the mantle (tilma) of Saint Juan Diego which has been faithfully venerated in her "sacred little house" (*Nican Mopohua*, no. 26) from the time of her apparitions to the present day.

When, after his first visit with the Bishop, Juan Diego begged Our Lady to choose another more efficacious messenger, Our Lady responded to him:

> Listen my youngest son, know for sure that I have no lack of servants, of messengers, to whom I can give the task of carrying my breath, my word, so that they carry out my will; but it is necessary that you, personally, go and plead, that by your intercession, my wish, my will, become a reality. (*Nican Mopohua*, nos. 58-59)

From Our Lady of Guadalupe, we, together with Saint Juan Diego, learn that we are called to become bearers of God, heralds of Christ, in the world. As bearers of God, we, like Saint Juan Diego, are servants of the Mother of God. Through the intercession of Our Lady of Guadalupe, may we become ever more her faithful servants, so that all of our brothers and sisters may know her as the Mother of God and may experience her unconditional maternal love for them, so that, through her maternal care, they may know, love, and serve her Divine Son.

NOVENA PRAYER *to* Our Lady *of* Guadalupe

O Virgin Mother of God, we fly to your protection and beg your intercession against the darkness and sin which ever more envelop the world and menace the Church. Your Son, Our Lord Jesus Christ, gave you to us as our mother as He died on the Cross for our salvation. So, too, in 1531, when darkness and sin beset us, He sent you, as Our Lady of Guadalupe, on Tepeyac to lead us to Him Who alone is our light and our salvation.

Through your apparitions on Tepeyac and your abiding presence with us on the miraculous mantle of your messenger, Saint Juan Diego, millions of souls converted to faith in your Divine Son. Through this novena and our consecration to you, we humbly implore your intercession for our daily conversion of life to Him and the conversion of millions more who do not yet believe in Him. In our homes and in our nation, lead us to Him Who alone wins the victory over sin and darkness in us and in the world.

Unite our hearts to your Immaculate Heart so that they may find their true and lasting home in the Most Sacred Heart of Jesus. Ever guide us along the pilgrimage of life to our eternal home with Him. So may our hearts, one with yours, always trust in God's promise of salvation, in His never-failing mercy toward all who turn to Him with a humble and contrite heart. Through this novena and our consecration to you, O Virgin of Guadalupe, lead all souls in America and throughout the world to your Divine Son in Whose name we pray. Amen.

MAY ∽ REFLECTION ONE

As the second month of our Nine-Month Novena to Our Lady of Guadalupe concludes, and as we, today, officially begin the third month, let us thank God and Our Lady for the grace of perseverance which that Our Lord, through the maternal mediation of Our Lady, has given to us so that we might fight the good fight, finish the race, and keep the Faith (cf. 2 Tim. 4, 7).

Our Lady commissioned Saint Juan Diego to be her heroic messenger, just as she commissions us today to lead others to Christ by handing on to them the truths of the Faith and its beauty in the life of prayer and, above all, of divine worship. However, after Bishop Juan de Zumárraga's initial skeptical reaction to Saint Juan Diego's account of Our Lady's desire, Saint Juan Diego considered himself to be unworthy of the mission that the Mother of God had entrusted into his hands. Saint Juan Diego was always docile and obedient, but, at the same time, he doubted that he could do all that God was asking of him. When the work seemed particularly difficult, he thought of reasons why the mission should be entrusted to someone else, and he even suggested to Our Lady that he was not the right person for her mission. Yet as a child is comforted by a mother's love, so too, Saint Juan Diego found comfort in Our Lady's words:

> I will reward the care, the work and the fatigue that you have put into this for me (*Nican Mopohua*, no. 92).

Our Lord Himself teaches us that God reveals His will to the "childlike" (Mt 11, 25), to those who, like Him, are "meek and humble of heart" (Mt 11, 29), to those who recognize that all that they are and have comes from the hand of God and who, therefore, place all their trust in Him. He assures us that, if doing His will demands much labor and is burdensome, He will "give [us] rest" (Mt 11, 28). Using an image from farming to describe our work with Him for the salvation of the world, he encourages us to "take [His] yoke" (Mt 11, 29) upon our shoulders. He declares: "For my yoke is easy, and my burden light" (Mt 11, 30).

In our daily struggle to be faithful and generous co-workers with Christ in His saving work, let us call upon the intercession of Our Lady of Guadalupe and her heroic messenger, Saint Juan Diego, even as we seek to follow their example. Christ will never fail us. He will render efficacious for our salvation and the salvation of the world our every good thought, word, and deed. When we are tempted to give up in the battle, let us bear in mind Our Lady's words to Saint Juan Diego for they are motherly words which will comfort and encourage us as well: "I will reward the care, the work and the fatigue that you have put into this for me."

NOVENA PRAYER *to* Our Lady *of* Guadalupe

O Virgin Mother of God, we fly to your protection and beg your intercession against the darkness and sin which ever more envelop the world and menace the Church. Your Son, Our Lord Jesus Christ, gave you to us as our mother as He died on the Cross for our salvation. So, too, in 1531, when darkness and sin beset us, He sent you, as Our Lady of Guadalupe, on Tepeyac to lead us to Him Who alone is our light and our salvation.

Through your apparitions on Tepeyac and your abiding presence with us on the miraculous mantle of your messenger, Saint Juan Diego, millions of souls converted to faith in your Divine Son. Through this novena and our consecration to you, we humbly implore your intercession for our daily conversion of life to Him and the conversion of millions more who do not yet believe in Him. In our homes and in our nation, lead us to Him Who alone wins the victory over sin and darkness in us and in the world.

Unite our hearts to your Immaculate Heart so that they may find their true and lasting home in the Most Sacred Heart of Jesus. Ever guide us along the pilgrimage of life to our eternal home with Him. So may our hearts, one with yours, always trust in God's promise of salvation, in His never-failing mercy toward all who turn to Him with a humble and contrite heart. Through this novena and our consecration to you, O Virgin of Guadalupe, lead all souls in America and throughout the world to your Divine Son in Whose name we pray. Amen.

MAY ∽ REFLECTION TWO

We consider Saint Juan Diego, heroic messenger of Our Lady of Guadalupe, as our model in showing forth the mercy of God in our homes, in our local communities, and in our world. At the same time, we call upon the help of his prayers, so that we may be able to carry out the Christian mission of merciful love with fidelity and generosity, as the Virgin of Guadalupe instructs us.

The best way to know Saint Juan Diego is to study the account of the apparitions of the Mother of God to him. The *Nican Mopohua*, the account of the apparitions written by Antonio Valeriano, a good friend of the Saint and a well-respected native-American scholar of the time, is the fruit of their many conversations about the apparitions. Saint Juan Diego dedicated the 17 years of his life after the apparitions to describing the apparitions and message of Our Lady to pilgrims to her "sacred little house" in which they could venerate her miraculous image on his tilma or mantle. His good and learned friend, Antonio Valeriano, never tired of hearing again from Saint Juan Diego the account of the visits of Our Lady to Tepeyac Hill from December 9th to 12th of 1531. He became a privileged messenger of Our Lady by employing his literary skills to hand on her message of Divine Love Incarnate as she communicated it to Saint Juan Diego.

In the *Nican Mopohua*, what is immediately evident is the intimacy of Saint Juan Diego's relationship with the Mother of God and, through her, with the Lord. Our Lady speaks to him in the most endearing terms, in the language of a mother for her child, and he responds, always with the greatest respect, in an equally affectionate manner. It is clear that his relationship with God, through the Virgin Mother, is the center of his life. In fact, when the Mother of God called upon him to be her trusted messenger to the Bishop and her trusted herald for pilgrims, he put all other concerns aside, until he had first accomplished what she was asking of him. His words to her, in their simple yet beautiful eloquence, inspire us:

> My Lady, my Queen, my Little Girl, let me not anguish you or grieve your face, your heart; truly with gladness I will go to carry out your venerable breath, your venerable word; I absolutely will not fail to do it, nor does the road trouble me. I will go now, to carry out your will (*Nican Mopohua*, nos. 63-64).

As we persevere in carrying out Our Lady's intention during this Nine-Month Novena and Consecration, let us pray that God, through the intercession of Our Lady of Guadalupe, will drive away from us, from the Church, and from the world all the influence of the Evil One. Satan makes bold to sow his lies, the seeds of confusion and destruction, especially within the Church. Let us pray, through the intercession of Our Lady of Guadalupe, that Christ Who alone is King of Heaven and of Earth may reign in our hearts, may reign throughout the world. Let our homes be, first and foremost, a place in which the image of the Sacred Heart of Jesus, Christ the King, symbolizes his rule over the hearts of all and inspires a life always more faithful to His grace at work within us for the salvation of the world. Let our homes be a place in which the image of the Immaculate Heart of Mary, the image of the Virgin of Guadalupe, draws every member of the household to the Sacred Heart of Jesus, the Divine Heart full of truth and love.

NOVENA PRAYER *to* Our Lady *of* Guadalupe

O Virgin Mother of God, we fly to your protection and beg your intercession against the darkness and sin which ever more envelop the world and menace the Church. Your Son, Our Lord Jesus Christ, gave you to us as our mother as He died on the Cross for our salvation. So, too, in 1531, when darkness and sin beset us, He sent you, as Our Lady of Guadalupe, on Tepeyac to lead us to Him Who alone is our light and our salvation.

Through your apparitions on Tepeyac and your abiding presence with us on the miraculous mantle of your messenger, Saint Juan Diego, millions of souls converted to faith in your Divine Son. Through this novena and our consecration to you, we humbly implore your intercession for our daily conversion of life to Him and the conversion of millions more who do not yet believe in Him. In our homes and in our nation, lead us to Him Who alone wins the victory over sin and darkness in us and in the world.

Unite our hearts to your Immaculate Heart so that they may find their true and lasting home in the Most Sacred Heart of Jesus. Ever guide us along the pilgrimage of life to our eternal home with Him. So may our hearts, one with yours, always trust in God's promise of salvation, in His never-failing mercy toward all who turn to Him with a humble and contrite heart. Through this novena and our consecration to you, O Virgin of Guadalupe, lead all souls in America and throughout the world to your Divine Son in Whose name we pray. Amen.

JUNE ☙ REFLECTION ONE

Great are the difficulties we are called to face in the Church and in the world. When such difficulties seem overwhelming, even prayer may appear to be one more difficulty, but that is a snare of Satan. The truth is that prayer, which is a union of our hearts with the glorious-pierced Heart of Jesus, is the balm of healing and strength in bearing all our burdens. The great test of our total dedication to the mission that we have taken up is to persevere for six more months as we pray for the conversion of the world.

The great test of Saint Juan Diego's total dedication to Our Lady came with the grave illness of his uncle, Juan Bernardino. It was after the second apparition on December 10th, during which Our Lady requested that he return the next day, December 11th, to receive from her the proof of the truth of the apparitions, which Bishop Juan de Zumárraga was requesting. He found his uncle mortally ill. He, therefore, remained at home with him for the entire day on December 11th. Early in the morning of December 12th, he was going to ask the priest to come to prepare his uncle for death. In order to prevent any delay in obtaining critical spiritual help for his dying uncle, he attempted to avoid an encounter with Our Lady. She, however, saw him and approached him, inquiring of his plans.

Saint Juan Diego explained the grave situation of his uncle to which he was attending, but, at the same time, he assured Our Lady that, as soon as the spiritual needs of his uncle had been met, he would return to complete the mission which she had entrusted to him.

In response, Our Lady reassured him that his uncle was already well. In fact, at the exact moment, just as she appeared to Saint Juan Diego, she also appeared to Juan Bernardino and she healed him of his illness. Our Lady's words of comfort to Juan Diego are words that should comfort us as well whenever we experience the temptation to doubt the importance and immediacy of carrying out all that Our Lady desires and has asked of us.

> Listen, put it into your heart, my youngest son, that what frightened you, what afflicted you is nothing; do not let it disturb your face, your heart; do not fear this sickness or any other sickness, nor any sharp or hurtful thing. Am I not here, I who have the honor to be your mother? Are you not in my shadow and under my protection? Am I not the source of your joy? Are you not in the hollow of my mantle, in the crossing of my arms? Do you need anything more? (*Nican Mopohua*, nos. 118-119)

Having received Our Lady's assurance, Saint Juan Diego carried out his mission immediately by returning once more to the Bishop, explaining to him the desire of the ever Virgin Mary for the building of a sacred little house and bringing to the Bishop the sign of the truth of Our Lady's message for him.

We, too, receive Our Lady's assurance in those same encouraging words: What afflicts you is nothing; do not let it disturb you; do not fear; she is here; she is your mother; she protects you; she is the source of your joy; she is holding you in her arms.

NOVENA PRAYER *to* Our Lady *of* Guadalupe

O Virgin Mother of God, we fly to your protection and beg your intercession against the darkness and sin which ever more envelop the world and menace the Church. Your Son, Our Lord Jesus Christ, gave you to us as our mother as He died on the Cross for our salvation. So, too, in 1531, when darkness and sin beset us, He sent you, as Our Lady of Guadalupe, on Tepeyac to lead us to Him Who alone is our light and our salvation.

Through your apparitions on Tepeyac and your abiding presence with us on the miraculous mantle of your messenger, Saint Juan Diego, millions of souls converted to faith in your Divine Son. Through this novena and our consecration to you, we humbly implore your intercession for our daily conversion of life to Him and the conversion of millions more who do not yet believe in Him. In our homes and in our nation, lead us to Him Who alone wins the victory over sin and darkness in us and in the world.

Unite our hearts to your Immaculate Heart so that they may find their true and lasting home in the Most Sacred Heart of Jesus. Ever guide us along the pilgrimage of life to our eternal home with Him. So may our hearts, one with yours, always trust in God's promise of salvation, in His never-failing mercy toward all who turn to Him with a humble and contrite heart. Through this novena and our consecration to you, O Virgin of Guadalupe, lead all souls in America and throughout the world to your Divine Son in Whose name we pray. Amen.

JUNE ∽ REFLECTION TWO

In my previous reflection, we considered how difficulties experienced in life can give rise to temptations to avoid the summons of Our Lady. When Saint Juan Diego's uncle, Juan Bernardino, became deathly ill, Juan Diego, seeking a priest to hear his uncle's confession and prepare his uncle's soul for death, tried to avoid a personal encounter with Our Lady, believing that her mission would delay his ostensibly noble cause. Yet, notwithstanding his intentions, she appeared to him and offered him her maternal consolation, assuring him with these words: "Am I not here, I who have the honor to be your mother?" and "Are you not in the hollow of my mantle, in the crossing of my arms?" (*Nican Mopohua*, no. 119) Our Lady assured her heroic messenger that his uncle would not die, that by fulfilling her desire he would also best care for his uncle.

Saint Juan Diego believed her, and his humble trust was more than rewarded, for the final message from Our Blessed Mother would be the capstone of Guadalupe and the heart of the conversion of millions of Native Americans and of the Spanish explorers and settlers. She told him to ascend to the rocky Hill of Tepeyac to gather roses in the winter. For his part, he immediately fulfilled her request, as the incontrovertible proof of Our Lady's appearances. The account tells us:

> And then Juan Diego climbed the little hill,
> and when he reached the top, he marveled
> at how many flowers were spread out there,

> their blossoms were open, flowers of every kind, lovely and beautiful, like those of Castille, when it was not yet their season because it was when the frost was worst. The flowers were giving off an extremely soft fragrance, like precious pearls, as if filled with the night's dew. Right away he began to cut them, gathered them all and put them in the hollow of his tilma. The top of the little hill was certainly not a place in which any flowers grew, because it was rocky, there were burs, thorny plants, prickly pear, and an abundance of mesquite bushes. And though some small grasses might grow, it was then the month of December, in which the ice eats everything up and destroys it (*Nican Mopohua*, nos. 127-133).

The miraculous flowers were but part of the reward of Saint Juan Diego's humble trust. God granted an even more remarkable and enduring sign of all that He wished to accomplish in His merciful love by leaving permanently the image of the Virgin of Guadalupe on Saint Juan Diego's Tilma. It was the Tilma that became both the miraculous proof of Our Lady's apparitions and the catalyst for the conversion of millions of souls.

Take Saint Juan Diego as your model in your every thought, word, and action, so that you may serve God in all things, both great and small. Commit yourselves to be, with the Mother of God, a messenger of God's merciful love in your homes, in your offices or schools, and in every place in which you find yourselves. Be humble, recognizing that all that you are and have comes from God. Be confident that, if you respect God's plan for you and for our world, you will be blessed, and you will bring a blessing to others.

As true children of God, with humility and confidence, like Saint Juan Diego, let us be one with the Virgin Mother of God in giving our hearts completely to the Lord. Calling upon the intercession of Saint Juan Diego, we pray for the humility to be always ready to do whatever God asks of us, and we pray for the trust that He will bring to a good conclusion our humble efforts to serve Him faithfully in even the smallest matters.

NOVENA PRAYER *to* Our Lady *of* Guadalupe

O Virgin Mother of God, we fly to your protection and beg your intercession against the darkness and sin which ever more envelop the world and menace the Church. Your Son, Our Lord Jesus Christ, gave you to us as our mother as He died on the Cross for our salvation. So, too, in 1531, when darkness and sin beset us, He sent you, as Our Lady of Guadalupe, on Tepeyac to lead us to Him Who alone is our light and our salvation.

Through your apparitions on Tepeyac and your abiding presence with us on the miraculous mantle of your messenger, Saint Juan Diego, millions of souls converted to faith in your Divine Son. Through this novena and our consecration to you, we humbly implore your intercession for our daily conversion of life to Him and the conversion of millions more who do not yet believe in Him. In our homes and in our nation, lead us to Him Who alone wins the victory over sin and darkness in us and in the world.

Unite our hearts to your Immaculate Heart so that they may find their true and lasting home in the Most Sacred Heart of Jesus. Ever guide us along the pilgrimage of life to our eternal home with Him. So may our hearts, one with yours, always trust in God's promise of salvation, in His never-failing mercy toward all who turn to Him with a humble and contrite heart. Through this novena and our consecration to you, O Virgin of Guadalupe, lead all souls in America and throughout the world to your Divine Son in Whose name we pray. Amen.

JULY ∽ REFLECTION ONE

Last month, our reflection focused on the trust that Saint Juan Diego placed in Our Lady of Guadalupe, even when difficult circumstances in his life tempted him to avoid a personal encounter with her, which she corrected with the love and mercy of a mother redirecting the faltering footsteps of her child.

This month, let us turn our attention to the last direction of the Virgin Mother of God, Our Lady of Guadalupe, which is that we are to become her messengers, just as she called Saint Juan Diego to be her messenger to Bishop Juan de Zumárraga. Juan Diego experienced numerous temptations from Satan to avoid Our Lady's mission. An early snare tempted him to excuse himself from the mission because he was the wrong person to carry it out, describing himself as "just a man from the country" and because he was not someone to approach the Bishop, declaring that the Bishop's residence "is not my place to go or to stay" (*Nican Mopohua*, no. 55).

All of us can easily give way to doubt and fear before the challenge of living in Christ in our totally secularized culture. There is the tendency to doubt God's grace and to give way to fear in responding to its "costly" demands. There is the temptation to think that we must devise some program, "some magic formula" (Pope Saint John Paul II, *Novo Millennio Ineunte*), to transform the world. Yet it is Christ, alive for us in the Church, Who alone shows us the way. It is our humble and confident following of Christ which will transform us and our world. To help us follow

Him, Our Lord, as He was dying upon the cross, gave us His Mother as our Mother.

By the mystery of the Divine Maternity, the Immaculate Heart of the Blessed Virgin Mary, assumed into glory, never ceases to beat with love for us, the children whom her Divine Son gave to her, as He was dying upon the Cross. When Our Lord pronounced the words, "Woman, behold thy son" (Jn 19, 26) to His Mother and "Behold thy mother" (Jn 19, 27) to Saint John the Apostle and Evangelist, standing at the foot of the cross, He expressed an essential reality of the salvation He was winning for us: the full cooperation of His Mother, the Blessed Virgin Mary, in His saving work. The Mother of God the Son Incarnate is the Mother of Divine Grace at work in our souls.

The work that the Virgin of Guadalupe gave to Saint Juan Diego is the work that Our Lord asks us to continue today: It is the work of evangelization in the Church and in the world. Her humbling words to Saint Juan Diego are her words to us, too: "I have no lack of servants, of messengers, to whom I can give the task" (*Nican Mopohua*, no. 58). The Queen of Heaven can choose anyone to accomplish her desire, but she, Our Blessed Mother, has chosen you and me, her children, to be her messengers, to carry the Word of God, her Divine Son, into the hearts of all, so that they might unite their heart to her Immaculate Heart, through whom our hearts become more intimately united to the Sacred Heart of Jesus. Accordingly, let her words to Saint Juan Diego fill us with virtuous courage as we persevere in this Nine-Month Novena. "I, personally, the ever Virgin Holy Mary, I, who am the Mother of God, sent you as my messenger" (*Nican Mopohua*, no. 62).

NOVENA PRAYER
to Our Lady *of* Guadalupe

O Virgin Mother of God, we fly to your protection and beg your intercession against the darkness and sin which ever more envelop the world and menace the Church. Your Son, Our Lord Jesus Christ, gave you to us as our mother as He died on the Cross for our salvation. So, too, in 1531, when darkness and sin beset us, He sent you, as Our Lady of Guadalupe, on Tepeyac to lead us to Him Who alone is our light and our salvation.

Through your apparitions on Tepeyac and your abiding presence with us on the miraculous mantle of your messenger, Saint Juan Diego, millions of souls converted to faith in your Divine Son. Through this novena and our consecration to you, we humbly implore your intercession for our daily conversion of life to Him and the conversion of millions more who do not yet believe in Him. In our homes and in our nation, lead us to Him Who alone wins the victory over sin and darkness in us and in the world.

Unite our hearts to your Immaculate Heart so that they may find their true and lasting home in the Most Sacred Heart of Jesus. Ever guide us along the pilgrimage of life to our eternal home with Him. So may our hearts, one with yours, always trust in God's promise of salvation, in His never-failing mercy toward all who turn to Him with a humble and contrite heart. Through this novena and our consecration to you, O Virgin of Guadalupe, lead all souls in America and throughout the world to your Divine Son in Whose name we pray. Amen.

JULY ∽ REFLECTION TWO

At her first apparition, on December 9th, 1531, Our Lady of Guadalupe favors and chooses as her heroic messenger Saint Juan Diego, a humble Christian who was on his way "to follow the things of God that are to us given, that are taught to us by our priests, those who are the images of the Lord, Our Lord" (*Nican Mopohua*, no. 24). That is, he was seeking to deepen his knowledge of the faith through instruction from the priest whom he acknowledges as an image of Christ alive for us in the Church. He gives expression to the truth that the priest, by virtue of the Sacrament of Holy Orders, acts in the person of Christ, Head and Shepherd of the flock in every time in every place. He shows us that only the truth, ultimately the Truth Who is Our Lord Jesus Christ alive for us in His holy Church, permits us to grow in holiness of life and thus to find joy and peace during the days of our earthly pilgrimage and their fullness at the destiny of our pilgrimage, the Kingdom of Heaven.

When Our Lady begins to speak with Saint Juan Diego, she immediately declares the truth of her being, of her relationship with God as Mother of God the Son Incarnate, and of her relationship with Juan Diego, as with all Christians. She declares:

> Know, know for sure my dearest and youngest son, that I am truly the ever perfect Holy Virgin Mary, who has the honor to be the Mother of the one true God for whom we all live, the Creator of

> people, the Lord of all around us and of what is close to us, the Lord of Heaven, the Lord of Earth (*Nican Mopohua*, no. 26).

What is primary for Our Lady in her relationship with Saint Juan Diego and in his collaboration as her messenger is the truth that she is the Virgin Mother of God the Son Incarnate Who is the King of Heaven and Earth and Who alone is our salvation.

Our Lady of Guadalupe equips us for today's grave crisis with the inseparable unity of truth and love. We cannot truly love another person while also disregarding or betraying the truth which should inform every relationship. The fundamental approach to the crisis of the family, of society, and of the Church is the knowledge of truth and the practice of it with love. Our Lady, when she requested the construction of a "sacred little house," informs us that the truth and love of her Divine Son, Jesus Christ, are found in His Mystical Body, the Church.

"I want very much that they build my sacred little house here, in which I will show Him, I will exalt Him upon making Him manifest, I will give Him to all people in all my personal love, Him that is my compassionate gaze, Him that is my help, Him that is my salvation.

> Because truly I am honored to be your compassionate mother, yours and that of all the people that live together in this land, and also of all the other various lineages of men; those who love me, those who cry to me, those who seek me, those who trust in me. Because there [at my sacred house] truly will I hear their cry, their sadness, in

> order to remedy, to cure all their various troubles, their miseries, their pains. (*Nican Mopohua*, nos. 26-32)

Our Lady does not propose some idea or some political action to address the various crises facing man. No, she proposes a person — the person of her Divine Son. She proposes the most intimate union of heart with His Most Sacred Heart as the only way to obtain mercy and ultimately eternal life. She tells Juan Diego that Christ is in fact her "compassionate gaze," even as He is her "help," her "salvation" (*Nican Mopohua*, no. 28).

In this way, too, she shows us that He, Jesus Christ, is the help that we are to offer to the world and to the Church in a time of great turmoil. As much as is possible, we desire that all people will see the Face of Christ and be drawn to Him Who alone can save them.

NOVENA PRAYER *to* Our Lady *of* Guadalupe

O Virgin Mother of God, we fly to your protection and beg your intercession against the darkness and sin which ever more envelop the world and menace the Church. Your Son, Our Lord Jesus Christ, gave you to us as our mother as He died on the Cross for our salvation. So, too, in 1531, when darkness and sin beset us, He sent you, as Our Lady of Guadalupe, on Tepeyac to lead us to Him Who alone is our light and our salvation.

Through your apparitions on Tepeyac and your abiding presence with us on the miraculous mantle of your messenger, Saint Juan Diego, millions of souls converted to faith in your Divine Son. Through this novena and our consecration to you, we humbly implore your intercession for our daily conversion of life to Him and the conversion of millions more who do not yet believe in Him. In our homes and in our nation, lead us to Him Who alone wins the victory over sin and darkness in us and in the world.

Unite our hearts to your Immaculate Heart so that they may find their true and lasting home in the Most Sacred Heart of Jesus. Ever guide us along the pilgrimage of life to our eternal home with Him. So may our hearts, one with yours, always trust in God's promise of salvation, in His never-failing mercy toward all who turn to Him with a humble and contrite heart. Through this novena and our consecration to you, O Virgin of Guadalupe, lead all souls in America and throughout the world to your Divine Son in Whose name we pray. Amen.

AUGUST ☙ REFLECTION ONE

In the economy of salvation, the Blessed Virgin Mary, crowned at her Assumption as Queen of Heaven and Earth, is the Mediatrix of All Grace. She, the first and best disciple of her Divine Son, cooperates fully in His Redemptive work from the moment of His conception to the moment of His death on the cross, when her Immaculate Heart was mystically pierced at the piercing of His Sacred Heart by the Roman soldier's spear. Always one in her glorious Immaculate Heart with His Most Sacred Heart, she continues, with maternal love, to be the channel of the immeasurable and unceasing graces that pour forth from His glorious-pierced Heart into the hearts of all the faithful. She is the Mother of Divine Grace.

Our Lady's work as Mediatrix became manifest with the establishment of a "sacred little house," a place of pilgrimage, in Tepeyac in 1531, whence she might show the mercy of God to all her children of America and of the world. As the great sign of her maternal desire to make us one with her Divine Son and, therefore, recipients of the immeasurable outpouring of God's mercy, God miraculously left her image on the Tilma or mantle of Saint Juan Diego. To this day, the Sacred Image, which has no human explanation as to its origin and whose fabric, cactus cloth, should have disintegrated some thirty to forty years after her apparitions, remains intact and radiates a miraculous maternal love.

Within eight years from the date of Our Lady's apparitions at Guadalupe, nearly nine million Native Americans converted to the Catholic faith, giving up the diabolical practice of human sacrifice and embracing the Christian way of life with remarkable fervor and fidelity. What is more, the European explorers and settlers and the Native Americans, who were on the verge of a most bloody conflict, united to form a new culture, the mestiza culture, which yet today looks to the Virgin of Guadalupe as its source and inspiration.

I have personally experienced her maternal love while gazing upon the Tilma. Through her maternal love, Our Lady of Guadalupe brings her children to her Divine Son, the only Savior of the world, in Whom we discover the wonder of our daily life, for God indeed dwells with us in the Church and within our souls.

When we come to her Shrine, Our Lady of Guadalupe, with deepest maternal affection, manifests to us the great mystery of God's love for us, inviting us to have complete confidence in His promises. Making our consecration to her, she draws us to encounter her Divine Son, the fulfillment of all of God the Father's promises. She draws us especially to the Sacraments of Penance and of the Most Holy Eucharist, so that we may know directly in our lives the fulfillment of God's promise of liberation from sin and death, His promise of eternal salvation. Making our consecration at the Shrine of Our Lady of Guadalupe will be our response to her pure and perfect love by totally giving our hearts to her Immaculate Heart, through whom we are ever more perfectly united to the glorious-pierced Heart of her Divine Son, Jesus the Savior.

NOVENA PRAYER *to* Our Lady *of* Guadalupe

O Virgin Mother of God, we fly to your protection and beg your intercession against the darkness and sin which ever more envelop the world and menace the Church. Your Son, Our Lord Jesus Christ, gave you to us as our mother as He died on the Cross for our salvation. So, too, in 1531, when darkness and sin beset us, He sent you, as Our Lady of Guadalupe, on Tepeyac to lead us to Him Who alone is our light and our salvation.

Through your apparitions on Tepeyac and your abiding presence with us on the miraculous mantle of your messenger, Saint Juan Diego, millions of souls converted to faith in your Divine Son. Through this novena and our consecration to you, we humbly implore your intercession for our daily conversion of life to Him and the conversion of millions more who do not yet believe in Him. In our homes and in our nation, lead us to Him Who alone wins the victory over sin and darkness in us and in the world.

Unite our hearts to your Immaculate Heart so that they may find their true and lasting home in the Most Sacred Heart of Jesus. Ever guide us along the pilgrimage of life to our eternal home with Him. So may our hearts, one with yours, always trust in God's promise of salvation, in His never-failing mercy toward all who turn to Him with a humble and contrite heart. Through this novena and our consecration to you, O Virgin of Guadalupe, lead all souls in America and throughout the world to your Divine Son in Whose name we pray. Amen.

AUGUST ↭ REFLECTION TWO

How does Our Lady propose that we know and serve her Divine Son Who alone is our salvation? Having announced to Saint Juan Diego the truth about herself and her relationship with God, and the truth about her Divine Son, Savior of the World, she asks that a chapel be built in which she will draw the faithful to encounter Him. She does not propose that he start a movement or some other initiative for the carrying out of Our Lady's mission, but rather that he ask Bishop Juan de Zumárraga to build a chapel:

> I want very much that they build my sacred little house here, in which I will show Him, I will exalt Him upon making Him manifest, I will give Him to all people in all my personal love, Him that is my compassionate gaze, Him that is my help, Him that is my salvation. (*Nican Mopohua*, nos. 26-28)

In what context does the Virgin of Guadalupe propose to teach us the mystery of God's ever faithful and all-merciful love? It is in the context of our entrance into the House of God to pray and to offer to Him the worship which He Himself inspires in us and strengthens us to carry out, under the maternal gaze of the Mother of God, especially looking lovingly upon us from the tilma, for she draws us to her Divine Son alive for us in the Church, above all, in the Sacraments of Penance and the Holy Eucharist. "I will show

Him," Our Lady of Guadalupe tells us by her apparitions, and "I will give Him to all people in all my personal love."

Being Our Lady's messengers, bringing people to her so that she can "show Him" and "give Him to all people," also means offering ourselves as channels of her maternal love, just as she is a channel of Divine Grace. Her image, which God miraculously left for us on the mantle, the tilma of Saint Juan Diego, makes visible the truth of the Virgin Mother's unique cooperation in Christ's work of Redemption. So, too, as her servants, as her messengers, we must make visible the truth of the Virgin Mother's work by, in a sense, wearing a spiritual Tilma for all the world to hear Christ through our words and see Him in our actions. In this, we offer all people her invitation to make a pilgrimage to her so that she can bring them to her Divine Son, since the ultimate goal of every pilgrimage to a shrine or holy place is to unite our hearts with His Most Sacred Heart, especially through the Eucharistic Sacrifice.

Our Lady makes clear that the mercy of God, incarnate in her Divine Son, is experienced by us in a preeminent way in the House of God, through prayer and divine worship:

> Because truly I am honored to be your compassionate mother, yours and that of all the people that live together in this land, and also of all the other various lineages of men; those who love me, those who cry to me, those who seek me, those who trust in me. Because there [at my sacred house] truly will I hear their cry, their sadness, in order to remedy, to cure all their various troubles, their miseries, their pains (*Nican Mopohua*, no. 29-32).

Accordingly, I invite you to make a pilgrimage to the Shrine of Our Lady of Guadalupe in La Crosse, Wisconsin, on December 12th, to consecrate your heart to the Most Sacred Heart of Jesus through the Immaculate Heart of the Virgin of Guadalupe, under the mosaic of Our Lady of Guadalupe, created by the artists at the Vatican Mosaic Studio to be a likeness of the image of Our Lady on the tilma.

NOVENA PRAYER *to* Our Lady *of* Guadalupe

O Virgin Mother of God, we fly to your protection and beg your intercession against the darkness and sin which ever more envelop the world and menace the Church. Your Son, Our Lord Jesus Christ, gave you to us as our mother as He died on the Cross for our salvation. So, too, in 1531, when darkness and sin beset us, He sent you, as Our Lady of Guadalupe, on Tepeyac to lead us to Him Who alone is our light and our salvation.

Through your apparitions on Tepeyac and your abiding presence with us on the miraculous mantle of your messenger, Saint Juan Diego, millions of souls converted to faith in your Divine Son. Through this novena and our consecration to you, we humbly implore your intercession for our daily conversion of life to Him and the conversion of millions more who do not yet believe in Him. In our homes and in our nation, lead us to Him Who alone wins the victory over sin and darkness in us and in the world.

Unite our hearts to your Immaculate Heart so that they may find their true and lasting home in the Most Sacred Heart of Jesus. Ever guide us along the pilgrimage of life to our eternal home with Him. So may our hearts, one with yours, always trust in God's promise of salvation, in His never-failing mercy toward all who turn to Him with a humble and contrite heart. Through this novena and our consecration to you, O Virgin of Guadalupe, lead all souls in America and throughout the world to your Divine Son in Whose name we pray. Amen.

SEPTEMBER ☙ REFLECTION ONE

When Our Lady provided Saint Juan Diego with the sign which the Bishop requested, she insisted on the importance of the chapel as the locus of the manifestation of God's all-merciful love:

> My youngest son, these different kinds of flowers are the proof, the sign that you will take to the Bishop; you will tell him from me that in them he is to see my wish and that therefore he is to carry out my wish, my will; and you, you who are my messenger, in you I place my absolute trust. And I strictly order you that only alone, in the Bishop's presence, will you open your tilma and show him what you are carrying; and you will tell him everything exactly, you will tell him that I ordered you to climb to the top of the little hill to cut the flowers, and everything you saw and admired; so that you can convince the Governing Priest, so that he will then do what is entrusted to him, to build my little sacred house that I have asked for. (*Nican Mopohua*, no. 137-142)

In fact, from the time of the apparitions of Our Lady of Guadalupe and the enshrinement of her miraculous image in the succession of chapels and churches built near Tepeyac

Hill, the devotion to Our Lady has favored a profound and rich life of prayer and divine worship.

In the end, everything regarding the apparitions is directed to the establishment of the chapel as a place of pilgrimage, of a privileged encounter with the Lord through the mediation of His Virgin Mother.

The presentation of the sign to Bishop Juan de Zumárraga is remarkable.

> And then he opened his white tilma, in the hollow of which were the flowers. And all the different flowers, like those from Castille, fell to the floor. Then and there his tilma became the sign, there suddenly appeared the Beloved Image of the Perfect Virgin Saint Mary, Mother of God, in the form and figure in which it is now, where it is preserved in her beloved little house, in her sacred little house in Tepeyac, which is called Guadalupe …
>
> And the Bishop got up, and untied Juan Diego's garment, his tilma, from his neck where it was tied, on which appeared the venerable sign of the Heavenly Queen. And then he took it and placed it in his private chapel. And Juan Diego still stayed for the day in the Bishop's house, who still kept him there. And on the next day he [the Bishop] said to him: "Come, let's go so you can show me where it is that the venerable will of the Queen of Heaven wants Her chapel built." (*Nican Mopohua*, nos. 181-184, and 188-192.)

If we are to be messengers of Our Lady, our hearts must be in union with her Immaculate Heart. Let us, therefore, build a "sacred little house" to Our Lady of Guadalupe in our hearts, setting a spiritual tilma in a place wherefrom, under the interior contemplation of her maternal gaze, she can prepare our hearts to make a pilgrimage to a holy place, where we can truly encounter her Divine Son, Jesus Christ, come to know Him more fully and to love Him more ardently, especially in the Sacraments of Penance and the Holy Eucharist.

I invite you on such a pilgrimage. At the Church of the Shrine of Our Lady of Guadalupe in La Crosse, Wisconsin, I encourage you to make the Solemn Act of Consecration to Our Lady of Guadalupe. The Shrine is a Vatican-approved place of pilgrimage, affiliated with the Basilica of Saint Mary Major in Rome and with the Basilica of Our Lady of Guadalupe in Mexico City. This affiliation means that those who come to the Shrine on pilgrimage receives the same graces and blessings as if they had gone on pilgrimage to the Basilica of Saint Mary Major or the Basilica of Our Lady of Guadalupe.

NOVENA PRAYER *to* Our Lady *of* Guadalupe

O Virgin Mother of God, we fly to your protection and beg your intercession against the darkness and sin which ever more envelop the world and menace the Church. Your Son, Our Lord Jesus Christ, gave you to us as our mother as He died on the Cross for our salvation. So, too, in 1531, when darkness and sin beset us, He sent you, as Our Lady of Guadalupe, on Tepeyac to lead us to Him Who alone is our light and our salvation.

Through your apparitions on Tepeyac and your abiding presence with us on the miraculous mantle of your messenger, Saint Juan Diego, millions of souls converted to faith in your Divine Son. Through this novena and our consecration to you, we humbly implore your intercession for our daily conversion of life to Him and the conversion of millions more who do not yet believe in Him. In our homes and in our nation, lead us to Him Who alone wins the victory over sin and darkness in us and in the world.

Unite our hearts to your Immaculate Heart so that they may find their true and lasting home in the Most Sacred Heart of Jesus. Ever guide us along the pilgrimage of life to our eternal home with Him. So may our hearts, one with yours, always trust in God's promise of salvation, in His never-failing mercy toward all who turn to Him with a humble and contrite heart. Through this novena and our consecration to you, O Virgin of Guadalupe, lead all souls in America and throughout the world to your Divine Son in Whose name we pray. Amen.

SEPTEMBER ☙ REFLECTION TWO

Although the apparitions of Our Lady of Guadalupe occurred nearly 500 years ago, Our Lord still desires that we continue coming to Our Lady of Guadalupe because He desires to speak to us through her as Mother of Divine Grace.

The situation today is no less urgent than it was at the time of the first apparitions. Our culture is plummeting at an alarming rate into self-annihilation. The situation in our own country is very frightening as the attacks on human life and on the family and on religious freedom grow ever more violent. Our society is radically unstable because we have lost our moorings. In other parts of the world, there are terrible conflicts, as there were during the time of Our Lady's apparitions. We realize that Our Lady's message is as critical today as it was then.

At the same time, Our Lady's remedy for the crisis of that time remains our own remedy today. She instructed that a "sacred little house" — that is, a chapel — be built. Knowing that it would be accomplished through Divine Providence, she prepared for her miraculous image on the tilma of Saint Juan Diego to be set in a place of prominence inside the chapel so that she might draw all who gaze upon that Sacred Image to her Divine Son. The description of the hanging of the tilma in her chapel deserves to be recounted.

And after some time, the Reverend Bishop moved the beloved Image of the Heavenly Maiden to the main church. He [the Bishop] took it from his palace, from his chapel where it had been, so that everyone could see and admire

Her precious Image. And absolutely everyone, the entire city, without exception, trembled when they went to behold, to admire Her precious Image. They came to acknowledge it as something divine. They came to offer Her their prayers. They marveled at the miraculous way it had appeared since absolutely no one on Earth had painted Her beloved Image. (*Nican Mopohua*, no. 212-218)

Our Lady is calling us to be her messengers today, just as she called Saint Juan Diego to be her heroic messenger 500 years ago. And just as the people were awestruck then, so too must people today tremble when they behold and admire her precious image. People must come to offer her their prayers. People need to marvel at the miraculous way her image appeared on the tilma! We can help them do so through the union of our hearts with the Immaculate Heart of Mary. Build a sacred little house in your heart. Contemplate her maternal gaze. Let her summon you on pilgrimage to a holy place where you will truly encounter her Divine Son in the Sacraments of Penance and Eucharist. Your example of living a holy life by supernatural grace will naturally lead others to Our Lady, who will draw them to the only source of their salvation in Jesus Christ, truly present in their midst.

I invite you to make a pilgrimage to the Shrine Church of Our Lady of Guadalupe at La Crosse, Wisconsin, where you can see her sacred image — a magnificent mosaic of the miraculous image on the tilma, created by the Vatican Mosaic Studio — which draws the attention of pilgrims to the altar of sacrifice, on which Our Lord makes sacramentally present His Sacrifice on Calvary, and to the tabernacle in which He remains for us as the Bread from Heaven. The crucifix which hangs above the altar of sacrifice, with the image of Our Lady as its background, reminds us that God the Son became incarnate in the Virgin Mary's womb, in order to offer His life for us on Calvary and to make that Sacrifice ever sacramentally present for us, until He returns in glory at the end of time. The Virgin of Guadalupe accomplishes her mission in her "sacred little house" in which her Divine Son dwells in the Most Blessed Sacrament.

You can see this image for yourself by making a pilgrimage to the Shrine of Our Lady of Guadalupe on this coming December 12th, the day of the Solemn Consecration, which will be the culmination of our Nine-Month Novena. Make the Official Act of Consecration to her. The Shrine has been approved by the Vatican to be an official place of pilgrimage by affiliating the Shrine with the Basilica of Saint Mary Major in Rome and with the Basilica of Our Lady of Guadalupe in Mexico City. Because of this affiliation, when you make your pilgrimage, you receive the same graces and blessings as if you had gone on pilgrimage to Rome, to the principal church dedicated to Our Lady in the universal Church, or to Mexico City, to the church in which the miraculous Tilma of Our Lady is enshrined.

NOVENA PRAYER
to Our Lady *of* Guadalupe

O Virgin Mother of God, we fly to your protection and beg your intercession against the darkness and sin which ever more envelop the world and menace the Church. Your Son, Our Lord Jesus Christ, gave you to us as our mother as He died on the Cross for our salvation. So, too, in 1531, when darkness and sin beset us, He sent you, as Our Lady of Guadalupe, on Tepeyac to lead us to Him Who alone is our light and our salvation.

Through your apparitions on Tepeyac and your abiding presence with us on the miraculous mantle of your messenger, Saint Juan Diego, millions of souls converted to faith in your Divine Son. Through this novena and our consecration to you, we humbly implore your intercession for our daily conversion of life to Him and the conversion of millions more who do not yet believe in Him. In our homes and in our nation, lead us to Him Who alone wins the victory over sin and darkness in us and in the world.

Unite our hearts to your Immaculate Heart so that they may find their true and lasting home in the Most Sacred Heart of Jesus. Ever guide us along the pilgrimage of life to our eternal home with Him. So may our hearts, one with yours, always trust in God's promise of salvation, in His never-failing mercy toward all who turn to Him with a humble and contrite heart. Through this novena and our consecration to you, O Virgin of Guadalupe, lead all souls in America and throughout the world to your Divine Son in Whose name we pray. Amen.

OCTOBER ☙ REFLECTION ONE

In what context does the Virgin of Guadalupe propose to teach us the mystery of God's ever faithful and all-merciful love? It is in the context of our entrance into the House of God to pray and to offer to Him the worship which He Himself inspires in us and strengthens us to carry out. "I want very much that they build my sacred little house here," Our Lady instructed the Church in Mexico through her messenger Saint Juan Diego. Her intention for the "sacred little house," the church, is to "show" her Divine Son, Jesus Christ, "exalt Him upon making Him manifest," and "give Him to all people" in her maternal love through prayer, devotion, and the Sacred Liturgy, especially the Sacraments of the Church (Cf. *Nican Mopohua*, no. 26-28).

In the Sacred Liturgy, Christ Himself acts in our midst for the glory of God and for our eternal salvation. In fact, it is only in the House of God that our greatest hunger and thirst are satisfied. In His dwelling with us through the Church, we know God in the forgiveness of our sins through the Sacrament of Penance and in the incomparable gift of the Body, Blood, Soul, and Divinity of Christ, the fruit of the Eucharistic Sacrifice given as Heavenly Bread to us in Holy Communion. Our Lady requests the building of a chapel or church because the Church's doctrine and discipline are the irreplaceable conditions for the encounter with Christ and the daily conversion of life to Christ by following Him on the only way which leads to eternal life, the way of the Cross (Cf. Mt 16, 24).

Mary, our Mother, preserved from all stain of Original Sin, understands better than any of us the wiles of Satan and the profound harm and eternal death itself, which come to us through sin. She witnessed the effects of the sin of our First Parents and of our actual sins in the Passion and Death of her Divine Son. She, therefore, stands ever ready to point out to us Satan's allurements and deceptions, and to sustain us in times of great trial and temptation by leading us to her Son alive for us in the Church, especially through the Sacraments of Penance and the Holy Eucharist. By drawing close to the Immaculate Heart of Our Blessed Mother, under the title of Our Lady of Guadalupe, we come to understand ever better the effects of sin in our lives and upon our world; we come to understand our need to go to her Son for the grace of conversion of life and the transformation of our world. In her maternal love, she leads us in the way of the humility which Our Lord teaches us in the Gospel, so that we give our hearts totally to Him, with confident trust in His never-failing and all-merciful love (Cf. Lc 9, 48).

The Shrine of Our Lady of Guadalupe in La Crosse, Wisconsin, was built to further the mission of Our Lady of Guadalupe, so that many more might know her maternal love and, through her love, know their Savior. In the planning and construction of the Church, every effort was made to reflect the ineffable beauty of God and of His faithful and enduring love of us, most especially in the Redemptive Incarnation of His only-begotten Son.

I invite you to come to the Shrine of Our Lady of Guadalupe on a pilgrimage on December 12, the Solemnity of Our Lady of Guadalupe, to make your Official Act of Consecration to her as the culmination of the Nine-Month Novena. Please tell others to come, too. Let them know that the Shrine is a Vatican-approved place of pilgrimage, affiliated with the Basilica of Saint Mary Major in Rome and the Basilica of Our Lady of Guadalupe in Mexico City. Let everyone know that those who come on pilgrimage to the Shrine receives the same graces and blessings as if they had gone on pilgrimage to those two great Basilicas.

NOVENA PRAYER *to* Our Lady *of* Guadalupe

O Virgin Mother of God, we fly to your protection and beg your intercession against the darkness and sin which ever more envelop the world and menace the Church. Your Son, Our Lord Jesus Christ, gave you to us as our mother as He died on the Cross for our salvation. So, too, in 1531, when darkness and sin beset us, He sent you, as Our Lady of Guadalupe, on Tepeyac to lead us to Him Who alone is our light and our salvation.

Through your apparitions on Tepeyac and your abiding presence with us on the miraculous mantle of your messenger, Saint Juan Diego, millions of souls converted to faith in your Divine Son. Through this novena and our consecration to you, we humbly implore your intercession for our daily conversion of life to Him and the conversion of millions more who do not yet believe in Him. In our homes and in our nation, lead us to Him Who alone wins the victory over sin and darkness in us and in the world.

Unite our hearts to your Immaculate Heart so that they may find their true and lasting home in the Most Sacred Heart of Jesus. Ever guide us along the pilgrimage of life to our eternal home with Him. So may our hearts, one with yours, always trust in God's promise of salvation, in His never-failing mercy toward all who turn to Him with a humble and contrite heart. Through this novena and our consecration to you, O Virgin of Guadalupe, lead all souls in America and throughout the world to your Divine Son in Whose name we pray. Amen.

OCTOBER ☙ REFLECTION TWO

Our Lady of Guadalupe's direction in 1531 was to build a "sacred little house," a chapel, a church, in order to draw people into a profoundly personal encounter with her Divine Son, Jesus Christ, in the Sacraments of Penance and Holy Eucharist. This is because she understands that the Church exists to call the culture to conversion and to transform it in accord with God's plan for us and for the world. She knows, too, that in the struggle to row the boat of the Church against the troubled waters of the confusion and error which surround us, there is the temptation to give up and to let the boat move with the times, with the result that the same confusion and error enters into the very life of the Church.

Yet God gave us the image of Our Lady on the Tilma, the mantle, of Saint Juan Diego, so that she would draw people drawn to see her, to her Divine Son, Jesus Christ. Our Lady assures us that, if we strive every day to give our lives completely to Christ, our great High Priest, Who has made us His brothers and sisters, then we can be confident that the turbulent waters which we are unable to navigate on our own become, with Christ, indeed navigable.

The purification and strength for our daily conversion of life and for meeting the challenge of teaching the truth of the faith and ministering the saving mysteries come solely from the Holy Eucharist, from our union with Christ in His Eucharistic Sacrifice and our communion with Him in His Body, Blood, Soul, and Divinity.

Contemplating her maternal gaze from the image of Our Lady of Guadalupe, we see the face of Christ and hear His invitation to unite our hearts to His Sacred Heart, and to unite our lives to His, and, with Mary, give our fiat — "be it done to me according to thy word" (Lk 1, 38) — to our mission, which is daily conversion of life to Jesus Christ, so that, by exercising His pure and selfless love, the world may be transformed into a civilization of love.

Come to the Shrine on December 12, the Solemnity of Our Lady of Guadalupe, to make your Official Act of Consecration. Unite your heart to the Sacred Heart of Jesus through the Immaculate Heart of Mary. Remember also that the Shrine has been approved by the Vatican as an official place of pilgrimage. Because of the Shrine's affiliation with the Basilica of Saint Mary Major in Rome and the Basilica of Our Lady of Guadalupe in Mexico City, the graces and blessings given to pilgrims at those Basilicas are also bestowed upon pilgrims who come on pilgrimage to the Shrine.

NOVENA PRAYER
to Our Lady *of* Guadalupe

O Virgin Mother of God, we fly to your protection and beg your intercession against the darkness and sin which ever more envelop the world and menace the Church. Your Son, Our Lord Jesus Christ, gave you to us as our mother as He died on the Cross for our salvation. So, too, in 1531, when darkness and sin beset us, He sent you, as Our Lady of Guadalupe, on Tepeyac to lead us to Him Who alone is our light and our salvation.

Through your apparitions on Tepeyac and your abiding presence with us on the miraculous mantle of your messenger, Saint Juan Diego, millions of souls converted to faith in your Divine Son. Through this novena and our consecration to you, we humbly implore your intercession for our daily conversion of life to Him and the conversion of millions more who do not yet believe in Him. In our homes and in our nation, lead us to Him Who alone wins the victory over sin and darkness in us and in the world.

Unite our hearts to your Immaculate Heart so that they may find their true and lasting home in the Most Sacred Heart of Jesus. Ever guide us along the pilgrimage of life to our eternal home with Him. So may our hearts, one with yours, always trust in God's promise of salvation, in His never-failing mercy toward all who turn to Him with a humble and contrite heart. Through this novena and our consecration to you, O Virgin of Guadalupe, lead all souls in America and throughout the world to your Divine Son in Whose name we pray. Amen.

NOVEMBER ꕥ REFLECTION ONE

At the Shrine of Our Lady of Guadalupe, we celebrate the mystery of God's dwelling with us in His only-begotten Son, conceived in the womb of the Blessed Virgin Mary, which the Virgin proclaimed from the moment of her first apparition to Saint Juan Diego on December 9th of 1531. It is the same mystery of God's immeasurable mercy and love toward us that Our Lady of Guadalupe announced in each of her apparitions over the three days which followed. It is the mystery which she never ceases to announce through her miraculous image which the hand of God Himself left for us on the mantle (tilma) of Saint Juan Diego on December 12th, the day of her final apparition. On that wonderful day, the Virgin provided to Bishop Juan de Zumárraga the sign of the truth of her apparitions, which he had requested from Saint Juan Diego: the miraculous flowering of roses in the middle of winter on a barren and stony hilltop. But, even more wonderfully, God provided the ultimate sign of that truth: He imprinted the image of the Virgin of Guadalupe on the mantle of Saint Juan Diego, so that, in a certain and true sense, she could continue to appear to His children who would come on pilgrimage to meet her and, in meeting her, to meet her Divine Son, above all in the Sacraments of Penance and the Most Holy Eucharist.

Coming to the Shrine on pilgrimage, the pilgrim leaves familiar surroundings to climb the Pilgrim Way leading to the Shrine Church out of a desire for a personal encounter with Our Lady, who draws us into an even more personal encounter with her Divine Son, Jesus Christ. The Virgin of Guadalupe brings us to meet her Divine Son in the Sacraments of Penance and the Holy Eucharist. The pilgrim indeed sees Our Lord, and encounters Our Lord, while praying in the Shrine Church before the Blessed Sacrament reposed in the tabernacle, in the Sacrament of Penance and, most wonderfully of all, through participation in the Eucharistic Sacrifice and in the reception of the incomparable fruit of that Sacrifice, the Body of Christ as the Heavenly Bread of our earthly pilgrimage.

The true pilgrim comes to the holy place with the deep desire for that personal encounter with Christ, to know Christ more and, therefore, to desire to encounter Him worthily in the Sacraments. The more pilgrims meet Christ in the Sacraments, the more they will want to love Him and to serve Him by bringing His love to their brothers and sisters, especially those who are in most need. Coming on pilgrimage to Our Lady of Guadalupe, so that she may lead us to her Son, Our Lord, we understand that communion with Him in sacred worship finds its ultimate expression in the truth and love according to which we conduct our daily lives. True worship of God inspires and strengthens us to do the will of God in all things. Ultimately, the pilgrimage attains its end when Christ has come to dwell in the heart of each pilgrim, in the pilgrim's home, through the mystery of His living presence with us in the Church.

I encourage you to make a pilgrimage to the Shrine of Our Lady of Guadalupe in La Crosse, Wisconsin, in order to offer your Act of Consecration to Our Lady of Guadalupe. However, should you be unable to undertake such a pilgrimage, I urge you to make your Act of Consecration in your parish church, in the presence of Our Lord reposed in the Most Blessed Sacrament, entrusting yourself with confidence to the loving intercession of the Mother of God.

NOVENA PRAYER
to Our Lady *of* Guadalupe

O Virgin Mother of God, we fly to your protection and beg your intercession against the darkness and sin which ever more envelop the world and menace the Church. Your Son, Our Lord Jesus Christ, gave you to us as our mother as He died on the Cross for our salvation. So, too, in 1531, when darkness and sin beset us, He sent you, as Our Lady of Guadalupe, on Tepeyac to lead us to Him Who alone is our light and our salvation.

Through your apparitions on Tepeyac and your abiding presence with us on the miraculous mantle of your messenger, Saint Juan Diego, millions of souls converted to faith in your Divine Son. Through this novena and our consecration to you, we humbly implore your intercession for our daily conversion of life to Him and the conversion of millions more who do not yet believe in Him. In our homes and in our nation, lead us to Him Who alone wins the victory over sin and darkness in us and in the world.

Unite our hearts to your Immaculate Heart so that they may find their true and lasting home in the Most Sacred Heart of Jesus. Ever guide us along the pilgrimage of life to our eternal home with Him. So may our hearts, one with yours, always trust in God's promise of salvation, in His never-failing mercy toward all who turn to Him with a humble and contrite heart. Through this novena and our consecration to you, O Virgin of Guadalupe, lead all souls in America and throughout the world to your Divine Son in Whose name we pray. Amen.

NOVEMBER ↭ REFLECTION TWO

Pilgrimage is among the most ancient spiritual practices, going back to the Old Testament. Our Lord Jesus Christ Himself went on pilgrimage with His Mother Mary and His Guardian, His Virginal Father, St. Joseph.

Every time we pray the Joyful Mysteries of the Rosary, we recall how Our Lord was left behind in Jerusalem at the conclusion of a pilgrimage from His hometown of Nazareth, and how Mary and Joseph found Him teaching the doctors of the law in the Temple.

Pilgrimage, in fact, is a deeply spiritual expression of the meaning of life itself, which is a journey from the moment of conception to the moment of death. On pilgrimage, we remember that here on earth we have no lasting city and that our days on earth, be they many or few, are a journey to the lasting home which Our Lord has prepared for us in Heaven (Cf. Jn 14:1-7; and Heb 13:14).

When we go on pilgrimage, we leave the familiar surroundings of our everyday life to journey to a holy place. What do we mean by a holy place? We mean a place in which Our Lord or His Blessed Mother or one of the saints has lived or appeared, or a place that has been set aside to the honor of Our Lord, His Blessed Mother, or one of the saints. At the holy place, a shrine or sanctuary is established, to which the faithful journey on pilgrimage.

Certain hardships are inherent to going on pilgrimage. In other words, a pilgrimage is not a tour or vacation but a spiritual time to be renewed in faith, hope, and charity. Often, reaching the location of the shrine or sanctuary requires special effort. Since most pilgrimages are made in company with other pilgrims, there is also the challenge to practice Christlike charity with our fellow pilgrims. We do not go on pilgrimage as angels but as frail human beings with all of our faults and failings which can try the patience of our fellow pilgrims.

Through daily Mass and the confession of sins in the Sacrament of Penance, pilgrims receive the extraordinary graces of the devotion of pilgrimage. At the Holy Mass, the pilgrim is reminded of the reason for his pilgrimage and receives the Body of Christ to sustain him on the pilgrimage. Through the Sacrament of Penance, the pilgrim seeks the forgiveness of his sins, of which he becomes conscious and for which he experiences deepest sorrow, as a particular grace of the pilgrimage.

At the Shrine of Our Lady of Guadalupe, the pilgrimage begins much like Saint Juan Diego with an ascent from the Pilgrim Center, up the hill, to the Shrine Church, drawn by Our Lady to seek a deeper life in Christ. You will first come to the Votive Candle Chapel, in which 700 candles lift up continuously the prayer intentions of the faithful. Ascending higher, you will encounter the statues of Saint Kateri Tekakwitha and Saint Joseph. At the top, in the plaza of the Shrine Church, you will see a statue of the final apparition with the figures of Saint Juan Diego and Bishop Juan de Zumárraga. Also from the plaza is the way to the Memorial to the Unborn, the Outdoor Stations of the Cross, and the Rosary Walk. At the crown of the façade of the Shrine Church is the figure of Christ the Good Shepherd, and of the Apostles Saints Peter, Prince of the Apostles, and Paul, Apostles of the Nations. Upon entering the church, you will see the narthex with the fresco of the entire story of Our Lady's apparitions. There are also side chapels of

Saint Gianna Beretta Molla, Blessed Miguel Pro, Saint Thérèse of Lisieux, Saint Faustina and the Divine Mercy, Saint Maria Goretti, and Saint Peregrine, each containing first-class relics of those saints. There are the confessionals as the privileged place of encounter with Christ for the forgiveness of our sins. In the transept are the statues of the Sacred Heart of Jesus and of the Immaculate Heart of Mary, and the statues of Saint Juan Diego and Saint Joseph with the Child Jesus. In the sanctuary are the crucifix, the altar with its baldacchino, and the tabernacle. At the heart of the sanctuary is the mosaic of Our Lady of Guadalupe above the tabernacle, drawing pilgrims to her Divine Son really present in the Holy Eucharist, in the Eucharistic Sacrifice and in its incomparable fruit, the Body of Christ as Heavenly Bread. Our Lady draws pilgrims to herself so that she may take them to Jesus Christ, Who alone is our salvation, in the Most Blessed Sacrament.

Through pilgrimage, pilgrims seek and receive, through the intercession of Our Lady and Saint Juan Diego, special graces in times of joy and sorrow for themselves, for their families, for the Church, and for the world. Indeed, pilgrimage leads to miracles and, in particular, to healing, both physical and spiritual. Thus, the goal of pilgrimage is to discover the extraordinary nature of our ordinary life because it is lived in Christ and is, indeed, a royal path leading to eternal life with God — Father, Son and Holy Spirit — in the company of all the angels and saints.

Once more, I encourage you, if at all possible, to make your Act of Consecration to Our Lady of Guadalupe at her Shrine in La Crosse, Wisconsin, undertaking a pilgrimage to this sacred place dedicated to her maternal solicitude. Should such a pilgrimage not be possible, I urge you to offer your Act of Consecration in your parish church, in the presence of Our Lord reposed in the Most Blessed Sacrament, entrusting yourself with filial confidence to the intercession of the Mother of God.

NOVENA PRAYER *to* Our Lady *of* Guadalupe

O Virgin Mother of God, we fly to your protection and beg your intercession against the darkness and sin which ever more envelop the world and menace the Church. Your Son, Our Lord Jesus Christ, gave you to us as our mother as He died on the Cross for our salvation. So, too, in 1531, when darkness and sin beset us, He sent you, as Our Lady of Guadalupe, on Tepeyac to lead us to Him Who alone is our light and our salvation.

Through your apparitions on Tepeyac and your abiding presence with us on the miraculous mantle of your messenger, Saint Juan Diego, millions of souls converted to faith in your Divine Son. Through this novena and our consecration to you, we humbly implore your intercession for our daily conversion of life to Him and the conversion of millions more who do not yet believe in Him. In our homes and in our nation, lead us to Him Who alone wins the victory over sin and darkness in us and in the world.

Unite our hearts to your Immaculate Heart so that they may find their true and lasting home in the Most Sacred Heart of Jesus. Ever guide us along the pilgrimage of life to our eternal home with Him. So may our hearts, one with yours, always trust in God's promise of salvation, in His never-failing mercy toward all who turn to Him with a humble and contrite heart. Through this novena and our consecration to you, O Virgin of Guadalupe, lead all souls in America and throughout the world to your Divine Son in Whose name we pray. Amen.

DECEMBER ∽ REFLECTION

May you have a most blessed Solemnity of Our Lady of Guadalupe.

We rejoice today as we make our Act of Consecration to Our Lady of Guadalupe, who, with deepest maternal love, brings her children to her Divine Son, the only Savior of the world. Since it is the Virgin of Guadalupe who has attracted us to this holy place in which indeed "God dwells on earth" (1 Kgs 8, 27), we, therefore, in a special way, venerate the Mother of God under her title of Our Lady of Guadalupe. As from all time, the Blessed Virgin Mary was chosen by God to be the instrument by which He would take our human flesh and remain with us always, so may she assist us who strive to serve Him.

The Act of Consecration to Our Lady of Guadalupe gives expression to the profound meaning of making a pilgrimage to a holy place. Through pilgrimage to a holy place we receive extraordinary grace for a deeper and more fervent relationship with Our Lord and His Blessed Mother. Pilgrimage effectively combats our tendency to become forgetful of God and of His law, and thus to allow the rebellion of sin to enter into our lives, two great spiritual evils which Satan, in his insidious way, is always trying to work upon us.

By the words of the Consecration, we articulate our desire to be one in heart with the Immaculate Heart of Mary in the Sacred Heart of Jesus. When our hearts, with the Immaculate Heart of Mary, rest totally in the Sacred Heart of Jesus, we become an instrument of untold graces for those who are in most need, an agent of the outpouring of divine love from the glorious pierced Heart of Jesus, and a sign of divine grace at work in our midst for the conversion of souls and the transformation of the world.

We place into Our Lady's Immaculate Heart the prayers of so many who have asked us to remember them in this holy place. We also ask the intercession of Mary Immaculate for our world and for the Church, which suffer deeply from pervasive confusion and error. We ask Our Lady of Guadalupe to intercede for the conversion of our personal lives and for the transformation of our culture which once was Christian but is increasingly pagan. In a particular way, we place into the Immaculate Heart of the Virgin Mother our profound concern for the restoration of respect for the inviolable dignity of innocent human life and for the integrity of the family, the cradle of human life.

Let us who have come on pilgrimage to the Shrine of Our Lady of Guadalupe or who are making their Act of Consecration elsewhere pray that all peoples throughout the world may unite their hearts always and more fully to the Immaculate Heart of Mary, who will not fail to bring our hearts to the glorious-pierced Heart of Jesus, her Divine Son. Let us pray that, through the intercession of Our Lady of Guadalupe and her faithful messenger, Saint Juan Diego, we will draw near to Our Lord in order to be, in the words of Saint Peter, "built into a spiritual house" (1 Pt 2, 5), offering worship to God "in Spirit and truth" (Jn 4, 24). Let us pray that, with Our Lady and Saint Juan Diego, we may be messengers of God's love and mercy to all, so that, in our faith and by our faithfulness, our brothers and sisters, and especially those whom the world considers the least among us (Cf. Mt 25, 40. 45), may have a profoundly personal encounter with the compassion of Our Savior,

Jesus Christ. Finally, let us also pray for the grace to remain always faithful in our service of the Lord during the days of our earthly pilgrimage until we reach its destiny, eternal joy and peace in His presence — Father, Son, and Holy Spirit — in the company of the angels and all the saints. May the Solemn Act of Consecration to Our Lady of Guadalupe be for us the program of our lives now and until we meet Our Lord in death and at the Day of His Final Coming.

May Our Lady of Guadalupe, Mother of America and Star of the New Evangelization, assist us to enthrone her Divine Son, Our Savior, in our hearts to reign there "now and at the hour of our death."

NOVENA PRAYER
to Our Lady *of* Guadalupe

O Virgin Mother of God, we fly to your protection and beg your intercession against the darkness and sin which ever more envelop the world and menace the Church. Your Son, Our Lord Jesus Christ, gave you to us as our mother as He died on the Cross for our salvation. So, too, in 1531, when darkness and sin beset us, He sent you, as Our Lady of Guadalupe, on Tepeyac to lead us to Him Who alone is our light and our salvation.

Through your apparitions on Tepeyac and your abiding presence with us on the miraculous mantle of your messenger, Saint Juan Diego, millions of souls converted to faith in your Divine Son. Through this novena and our consecration to you, we humbly implore your intercession for our daily conversion of life to Him and the conversion of millions more who do not yet believe in Him. In our homes and in our nation, lead us to Him Who alone wins the victory over sin and darkness in us and in the world.

Unite our hearts to your Immaculate Heart so that they may find their true and lasting home in the Most Sacred Heart of Jesus. Ever guide us along the pilgrimage of life to our eternal home with Him. So may our hearts, one with yours, always trust in God's promise of salvation, in His never-failing mercy toward all who turn to Him with a humble and contrite heart. Through this novena and our consecration to you, O Virgin of Guadalupe, lead all souls in America and throughout the world to your Divine Son in Whose name we pray. Amen.

ACT OF CONSECRATION *to* Our Lady *of* Guadalupe

DECEMBER 12

O Holy Virgin Mary, Mother of God and my compassionate Mother,[1] I, with Saint Juan Diego, your faithful and courageous messenger, prostrate myself before your Beloved Image.[2] With all my heart, I, too, desire to be your messenger. With Saint Juan Diego, may my heart be totally one with your Sorrowful and Immaculate Heart, perfectly united to the glorious-pierced Heart of your Divine Son, Our Lord and Savior Jesus Christ.

Conscious of my sins, of the evils oppressing the world and threatening the Church, and of the unrelenting guile of Satan, "the father of lies,"[3] I come before you, seeking your protection and invoking your intercession, that I may belong totally to your Divine Son, King of the Universe and King of my heart. Incarnate in your womb at Nazareth and born of you at Bethlehem, He came into the world to save me from sin and everlasting death. Obtaining my eternal salvation by His death on the Cross, He gave you to me to be my mother forever.[4] As His Mother, bring Him to me, and, as my Mother, bring me to Him Who alone is "the way, the truth, and the life,"[5] teaching me, as you taught the wine stewards at the Wedding Feast of Cana: "Do whatever He tells you."[6]

Before the troubles, the miseries, and the pains which afflict me, the world, and the Church,[7] I am tempted to give way to discouragement and to claim helplessness.[8] In moments of temptation, remind me that you have chosen me to be your messenger and that Our Lord, without measure and without cease, sustains with the sevenfold grace of the Holy Spirit a humble and contrite heart.[9] Help me to remain, with you, one in heart with the Sacred Heart of Jesus, trusting that God's promises to me will indeed be fulfilled.[10] Keeping me "in the hollow of your mantle" and "in the crossing of your arms,"[11] let no trouble, no misery, no pain obscure or diminish my service as your faithful messenger. Rather, with maternal love, encourage and strengthen me to take up steadfastly and joyfully the cross of pure and selfless love, which is indeed my only hope, my only way to joy and peace here and now, and to its fullness in the eternal life of Heaven.[12]

Under your protection and through your intercession, may I, every day and at every moment of the day, give myself anew to Jesus, "my Lord and my God,"[13] and may I, with you, draw to Him the many who do not yet know Him and the many who have known Him but are now far away from Him. Please intercede for me, that, through my conversion of life to Him and through His grace at work in my heart, my every thought, attitude, word, and action may attract others to Him Who alone is their salvation. Please intercede for my family and my homeland, that Christ the King may rule in all hearts from His Most Sacred Heart, pierced by the soldier's spear as He died on Calvary and now seated in eternal glory at the right hand of the Father, dispelling all darkness, all sin, and all attraction to sin.

O Virgin Mother of God and my compassionate Mother,

prostrate before your Beloved Image, I now unite my heart forever to your Sorrowful and Immaculate Heart, finding my true and lasting home in the Most Sacred Heart of Jesus. I consecrate myself to you, the Perfect Virgin, Saint Mary of Guadalupe.[14] I promise to be your ever faithful and courageous messenger on earth. Thus, at the end of my earthly pilgrimage, may I be forever in your company, together with the angels and all the saints, praising and glorifying God – Father, Son, and Holy Spirit. Please accept my Act of Consecration and never let me betray the gift of myself to you which, today, I make with all my heart. Amen.

---

[1] *Nican Mopohua*, nos. 26 and 29.

[2] *Nican Mopohua*, no.183.

[3] Jn 8, 44.

[4] Cf. Jn 19, 26-27.

[5] Jn 14, 6.

[6] Jn 2, 5.

[7] Cf. *Nican Mopohua*, no. 32.

[8] Cf. *Nican Mopohua*, nos. 54-56 and 111-116.

[9] Cf. Is 57, 15.

[10] Cf. Lk 2, 45.

[11] *Nican Mopohua*, no. 119.

[12] Cf. Mt 10, 38; 16, 34; Mk 8, 34; Lk 9, 23; Jn 12, 25-26.

[13] Jn 20, 28.

[14] *Nican Mopohua*, no. 208.

DAILY PRAYER *of* THOSE CONSECRATED *to* Our Lady *of* Guadalupe

Prayed from December 13th to March 11th of the following year.

O Virgin Mother of God, Our Lady of Guadalupe, at the beginning of a new day, I renew my consecration to you, my compassionate mother. I pray that, today, I, with Saint Juan Diego, may be your ever faithful messenger.

Please intercede for the conversion of my heart to Christ, your Divine Son. Throughout this day, may my heart, one with your Sorrowful and Immaculate Heart, rest ever more perfectly in His glorious-pierced Heart. In all things, may I do what He is asking of me. In difficulties, trials, and temptations, may I, in the embrace of your arms, trust His promise to win in me the victory over sin and death.

I pray also for the many who have abandoned Christ and for the many who do not yet know Him. May you bring millions of souls to Christ, and may I, your messenger, draw souls to Him Who alone is our salvation.

O Lady of Guadalupe, I place within your mantle my family and my homeland, asking that Christ may reign in all hearts from His Most Sacred Heart. At your pleading, may He pour forth into humble and contrite hearts the sevenfold gift of the Holy Spirit dispelling from them all darkness and sin, and inflaming them with divine truth and love.

May I, alive in Christ, advance today on the earthly pilgrimage to my lasting home with you and with the angels and all the saints, where we shall forever praise and glorify God – Father, Son, and Holy Spirit. With all my heart, I ask this in Christ, your Divine Son, my Lord and my Savior. Amen.

Por devocion de Dn Juan Baptista Eche

APPENDIX

MULIERIBUS ET
VENTRIS TUI IESUS SANCTA

EXCERPT
from
The SHRINE *of* OUR LADY *of* GUADALUPE
by
RAYMOND LEO CARDINAL BURKE

The following text is drawn from ***The Shrine of Our Lady of Guadalupe****, written entirely by Raymond Leo Cardinal Burke. In this work, His Eminence recounts the spiritual inspiration, historical development, and theological purpose of the Shrine in La Crosse, Wisconsin, dedicated to Our Lady of Guadalupe, Mother of America and Star of the New Evangelization.*

The excerpt included here presents Cardinal Burke's own welcome to pilgrims and his reflection on the meaning of pilgrimage, Marian devotion, the Sacred Liturgy, and the renewal of the family as the domestic church. It offers both a spiritual introduction to the Shrine and a personal testimony of faith that shaped its founding.

The complete text may be found in ***The Shrine of Our Lady of Guadalupe*** *by Raymond Leo Cardinal Burke. Pilgrims who desire a deeper understanding of the Shrine's mission and history are encouraged to consult the full volume.*

WELCOME

Dear Pilgrim,

A heartfelt welcome to the Shrine of Our Lady of Guadalupe! You have journeyed to a holy place, dedicated to our Savior and His Immaculate Virgin Mother, under her title of Our Lady of Guadalupe. Whether your pilgrimage is for an hour, a day, or even several days, may it deepen your knowledge of and your confidence in God's never-failing and immeasurable mercy and love toward you and all for whom you pray in this holy place.

The Shrine of Our Lady of Guadalupe was founded so that the Mother of God might speak to more and more of her children of America, as was her expressed ardent desire during her apparition to Saint Juan Diego at Tepeyac Hill on December 9, 1531. Through your pilgrimage, may the Mother of God speak to your heart. Through her maternal love, may you discover anew the great mystery of God's mercy and love at work in your daily life.

Not unlike Saint Juan Diego who ascended Tepeyac Hill, you will ascend from the Pilgrim Center up a small hill along the Pilgrim Way, in the direction of the Shrine Church. Along the Pilgrim Way is the Mother of Good Counsel Votive Candle Chapel, an outdoor devotional area dedicated to Saint Kateri Tekakwitha and another dedicated to Saint Joseph the Workman. In time, other devotional areas will be added, for example, an area dedicated to Saint Michael the Archangel, and an area dedicated to Saint Isidore the Farmer and his wife Saint Maria de la Cabeza.

The Pilgrim Way culminates in the plaza of the Shrine Church. In front of the church is a statue of the final apparition of Our Lady of Guadalupe on December 12, 1531, depicting the figures of Saint Juan Diego and Bishop Juan de Zumárraga. On the church façade are statues of Christ the Good Shepherd and of the Apostles Saints Peter and Paul. To the right of the plaza is Our Lady of Prémontré Priory with its chapel dedicated to Blessed John Duns Scotus. To the left of the plaza is the Memorial to the Unborn, the outdoor Stations of the Cross, and the Rosary Walk.

Inside the Shrine Church is the narthex where there is a fresco on the ceiling illustrating the entire story of Our Lady's apparitions. In the body of the Church are side chapels of Saint Gianna Beretta Molla, Blessed Miguel Pro, Saint Thérèse of Lisieux, Saint Faustina and the Divine Mercy, Saint Maria Goretti, and Saint Peregrine Laziosi. Near the sanctuary are statues of the Sacred Heart of Jesus, the Immaculate Heart of Mary, Saint Joseph with the Child Jesus, and Saint Juan Diego. Inside the sanctuary is the altar with its baldacchino, the crucifix over the altar, the tabernacle, and the mosaic of Our Lady of Guadalupe who draws us to Christ in His Real Presence in the Most Blessed Sacrament.

More details about these various areas of devotion and meditation at the Shrine are provided throughout this book.

Also, the staff and volunteers of the Shrine will assist you in every way possible, so that the Mother of God may lead you to her Divine Son with the loving instruction: "Do whatever He tells you" (Jn 2, 5). Please let them know how they may help you to receive abundantly the special graces which our Lord gives to pilgrims of this holy place.

Guided by Our Lady of Guadalupe, Mother of America and Star of the New Evangelization, please pray for our nation and its people, that, obedient to God's Word, it may overcome the culture of death and build up a civilization of life and divine love. Please pray, too, for the Church, that her members may faithfully and generously carry out the works of the New Evangelization. Finally, I ask you to pray for God's blessing upon the Shrine of Our Lady of Guadalupe that it may evermore be for pilgrims a place of encounter with Our Lord, under the care of His Virgin Mother.

May your pilgrimage bring you to the loving arms of the Mother of God and, through her intercession, to the Heart of her Son, God the Son incarnate in her womb.

The INSPIRATION *for the* SHRINE

The founding of the Shrine of Our Lady of Guadalupe was an answer to the summons by Pope Saint John Paul II for a new evangelization, a demand that we teach, celebrate, and live our Catholic faith with the engagement and energy of the first disciples of Our Lord, and of the first missionaries to our native place. As the saintly Pontiff frequently reminded us, the fruit of a new evangelization, the civilization of love, is first realized in the family, and it is only through the family that the whole of society is transformed. It is in the family that we first meet Christ, learn about God's love for us in Jesus Christ, are formed in the life of prayer, devotion and worship, and first experience and give the witness of Christ-like love. The transformation of the family is the way of the transformation of the whole of society.

With this in mind, the effort for the new evangelization focused on an effort to renew the devotional life of families and individuals, and to reinforce more effectively the Christian home as a little Church, the domestic Church in which God dwells with His people, and in which we first come to know God, we first pray, and we are first schooled in the Christian virtues. The family experiences its deepest reality and its strongest bond of unity when it is at prayer, especially at divine worship. From prayer and divine worship, every aspect of the personal life of each member of the family and of the family itself flows. The family at prayer and at worship manifests Christ alive in the Church most powerfully and, therefore, attracts many other families to Christ in His holy Church.

To provide a clearer picture of the inspiration to begin this work of a new evangelization, focusing on the family and culminating in the development of the Shrine dedicated to Our Lady, the Star of the New Evangelization, Queen of the Americas, the Blessed Virgin of Guadalupe, allow me now to share with you a brief reflection on my own family and upbringing, since, for me, from my earliest memories, my family was the first place in which I was taught, lived and witnessed the Catholic faith.

My father's family had emigrated from Ireland to the United States of America in the 1800s. They brought with them a strong Catholic faith which inspired a true spirituality in the home. The home, in fact, was seen as a little church, an extension of the parish church.

My mother's family had emigrated much earlier from England and were Protestant. When my mother married my father, she was attracted to the Catholic faith and received instructions from an outstanding Irish priest, Father Bernard McKevitt, who was the parish priest of my father's home parish, Assumption of the Blessed Virgin Mary Parish in Richland Center, Wisconsin. Thanks be to God and to Father McKevitt, my mother knew the Catholic faith thoroughly and was a strong part in the Catholic upbringing of my brothers and sisters, and me.

During those years of my childhood in the 1940s and 50s, my parents loved the Church and expressed that love, in a particular way, by their respect for the parish priest, for the parochial vicars, as well as for a good number of religious sisters who taught in the parish school. The priests were spiritual fathers to us children and the Sisters were spiritual mothers. They seemed to me to be an extension of the love of my parents.

Also during those years, the image of the Sacred Heart was enthroned in a prominent place in my home. The Sacred Heart of Jesus was the point of reference for our life as a family. All of us knew very strongly that Jesus was part of our family, living with us as though through an extension of the Real Presence in the Most Holy Eucharist offered on the altar of our parish church and reposed in the tabernacle after the Eucharistic Sacrifice. The Sacred Heart was the stable guest in our home, as He was also the stable guest of our hearts through the Indwelling of the Holy Spirit.

Our devotion to the Sacred Heart of Jesus was strongly linked to Eucharistic devotion and devotion to the Blessed Virgin Mary, especially under her title of Our Lady of Lourdes. In our parish, there was a strong devotion to the Sorrowful Mother, as promoted by the Redemptorist Fathers who also gave our regular parish mission. We frequently took part in the Sorrowful Mother Novena Devotion on Friday evenings, which always concluded with Benediction of the Blessed Sacrament. As a child and young man, I also always received a great consolation from the devotion to our Blessed Mother, venerated under the titles associated with her apparitions. From instruction that my siblings and I received at home and in my parish, I learned the important lesson that, in the effort to follow Christ faithfully, to be of one heart with Him, it is the Blessed Mother who faithfully guides us, consoles us when we encounter challenges and difficulties, and encourages us when we have failed.

My parents were dairy farmers. They impressed upon us children a sense of responsibility toward those who would be eating dairy products produced from the milk of our farm. Truly, I was taught to take a certain just pride in cooperating with nature, and, therefore, with God, to provide an important source of food for others. My parents also taught us children always to remember that we, as farmers, were working with God, in a direct way, and, therefore, to count upon His Divine Providence in all things. In that way, the importance of the Catholic faith was evident to us all. There was the sense of needing to be close to God, if we were to work effectively with Him and truly serve others. Special importance was attributed to the Rogation Days in the Spring, during which special prayers were addressed to God to bless the fields and farm animals, and all the instruments of the farmer's work. In the same way, the Ember Days were important to seek God's blessing upon the harvest, in order that it be bountiful and that we could gather it effectively for our good and the good of our neighbors. These days were filled with a deep thanksgiving to God, even as they were filled with wonder at the goodness of the harvest.

The greatest lesson that my parents taught us children was the centrality of Holy Mass on Sundays and on holy days of obligation as the highest and most perfect expression of our Catholic life and as the principal font of blessing for us as individuals and for our work. Sundays and holy days of obligation were also observed as days of rest. They were the special days when relatives and friends visited. Saturday always included preparation for Sunday Mass. We had special clothes and shoes for Sunday Mass which we had to make sure were ready, as well as making sure that we ourselves were prepared.

The family Rosary was a strong part of our daily life. It was the way in which we nurtured a strong sense of the presence of Our Lord in our lives through the mediation and intercession of Our Lady and of all the saints. The various mysteries of the Rosary helped us to understand more fully what it means to live in Christ, to have the gift of Christ's life within us individually and within the whole Church.

Special times of the year were marked with special devotions. During Advent, there was the practice of the Advent Wreath. During May, a special altar devoted to the Blessed Virgin Mary was placed in the living room. I recall how delighted we children were to pick beautiful wildflowers and lilacs, which were abundant in the springtime of the year in Wisconsin, and to bring them to adorn the May Altar of the Virgin Mother of God and so to honor her as our Blessed Mother, too. Lent was marked by a more penitential meal on the Fridays, especially Good Friday. Good Friday and Holy Saturday were especially quiet to honor the Death and Burial of Our Lord. Holy Saturday involved making special preparations for the celebration of Easter Sunday.

Around the dinner table, my father used to give us important lessons in good manners and in the human virtues. There was also a strong emphasis on how to act when visiting others. I recall going with my parents to visit the homes of friends and neighbors, and knowing to be quiet and respectful. I also learned from my parents the importance of showing hospitality to others who visited us. It always impressed me to see how immediately my parents would organize hospitality for unexpected visitors.

My father became gravely ill in 1955. He was eventually diagnosed with a brain tumor. An operation was performed to remove part of the tumor, but it was located in a place in which the tumor could not be completely removed. He was hospitalized from time to time but eventually came home to die. Although it was a very sad time, Our Lord used it to teach the whole family more fully the sacredness of human life and its ultimate destiny with Him in Heaven. One particularly moving experience was the visits of our parish priest, Father Owen Mitchell, to hear my father's confession and to bring him Holy Communion. I was particularly impressed because I had begun my own preparation for First Confession and First Holy Communion on May 11, 1956. My father's condition worsened. In those days, when the priest arrived at the door, the whole family met him with a lighted candle and led him to my father's room. We would then all leave the room so that the priest could hear my father's confession. After his confession, we would enter the room again, to be present for his reception of Holy Communion. Somehow, even as a child, I understood that it was Our Lord Who was sustaining my father and that, in dying, my father was preparing to meet Our Lord and to be with Him forever. In the midst of our sorrow as a family, these moments of strong grace brought us peace and joy.

When the day came for my First Holy Communion, my father was not well enough to join us at the church, but as soon as we returned home, my mother took me to his room. He had not been able to speak very much at all for some time. As soon as he saw me, he smiled. And it became so clear to me how important it was for him that I had received Our Lord in Holy Communion. Though his illness had weakened him greatly, he was able to say a few words: "I am very proud of you today." Two months later, my father died. Receiving the Sacraments were seen as the major events of our lives. Regular confession was a part of family life. The whole family would go to the parish church on Saturday afternoon for confession.

The most beautiful thing about my elementary school education was beginning every morning with the Holy Mass. This was the heart of our day; that much was clear to my family and me. After the High Mass on Sunday, there was Benediction of the Blessed Sacrament. There were also the Forty Hours Devotions and other times of Exposition and Benediction of the Blessed Sacrament. As I mentioned, our parish church in Richland Center, Wisconsin, had a special bond with the Redemptorist Fathers who conducted the regular parish mission. Every Friday evening, there was the Sorrowful Mother Devotion, promoted by the Redemptorists, which concluded with Benediction of the Blessed Sacrament.

Because it was clear that the first goal of my education was the knowledge of my vocation, my parents, priests, religious Sisters and Brothers, and other devout lay faithful encouraged me and all children to consider whether Our Lord might be calling us to the priesthood or to the consecrated life. It was a healthy practice at the time, since it led us to reflect upon these vocations in relationship to the vocation of our parents in the married life. For that reason, my mother and father recognized the need for early catechesis. In that regard, the *Baltimore Catechism* was a great blessing. Today, I recall the words of the truths of the faith, as we memorized them.

For me, learning deeply the truths of the faith and participation in the Sacred Liturgy daily were great gifts, and they did a great deal of lasting good for me. For example, as a child, learning the word "Transubstantiation" did not mean that I understood it fully, but, at the time, it was enough for me to grasp that it was not an everyday word or event. In time, my understanding of these formative catechetical teachings deepened, and difficult theological words like "Transubstantiation" remained the constant which has continued to draw me into deeper understanding and devotion. Thus, as a youngster, it was clear to me that the Holy Mass was the greatest gift given from the Heart of Jesus. The care with which one prepared for participation in the Holy Mass by the regular confession of sins and even by the simple but significant gesture of dressing in "Sunday clothes" all pointed to Holy Mass and, above all, Holy Communion as the most privileged and most perfect meeting with Christ mysteriously and really present for us in the Church.

Serving the Holy Mass, from the time I was in the fourth grade, deepened greatly my appreciation of the greatest mystery of our faith. In a very profound way, all of these different aspects of childhood instilled in me an ever more profound appreciation of truth, goodness and beauty in the contemplation of their source, God Who Is, the Being of God.

All of what I have been describing was of incalculable help to me in knowing and embracing my vocation in life. I thank God that my parents understood their irreplaceable role in my vocation. I thank God, too, for parish priests who understood their irreplaceable role in fostering vocations, especially vocations to the priesthood and the consecrated life. My family and home parish and school, and the work of the family farm, truly provided for me an education in the Gospel of Life and Divine Love. Although there were moments of great challenge, trial and suffering, God provided for my family and me deep joy and peace in our knowledge, love and service of Him.

All that my family gave to me came with me as I entered the diocesan minor seminary, Holy Cross Seminary in La Crosse, Wisconsin, in the Fall of 1962, which coincided with the beginning of the first session of the Second Vatican Ecumenical Council.

At that time, the seminary was filled to overflowing with seminarians. Upon entering, I was issued a personal copy of the *Liber Usualis* so that some hours each week could be devoted to perfecting the singing of Gregorian Chant, especially to learning the proper chants for each Sunday and Feast.

Those early years of seminary formation seemed like a time of tranquility. Yet within five years, the seminary underwent, in a particularly devastating manner, the crisis which the Church experienced during the first years of the implementation of the teachings of the Second Vatican Ecumenical Council. The implementation sadly took a very man-centered approach, with many strange ideas about making the Liturgy "interesting." (It almost seems blasphemous to me to say that we need to make the Liturgy *interesting*. What could be more interesting in itself and more compelling than the knowledge that the Sacred Liturgy is the gift of God's own encounter with us?) Many seminarians abandoned the praying of the Rosary, saying that this was the type of prayer Our Lord condemned as "rattling on" (Mt 6, 7), or that, if you prayed the Rosary, you did not have a proper appreciation for the Mass and for the other liturgical actions of the Church. The *Liber Usualis* was also suddenly and totally abandoned, and Gregorian Chant was replaced, in great part, by songs developed according to the standards of popular music and accompanied by the guitar and percussion instruments. Many riches of our life in Christ in the Church, which had developed along the Christian centuries, and which had been so important to my family and me, were abruptly and sometimes violently called into question, ridiculed, repudiated and cast aside.

In a very short period of time, places for the celebration of the Sacred Liturgy, Sacred Architecture, suffered a great decline, and also Sacred Music. Indeed, the true reform desired by the Council Fathers was frequently betrayed and must now be studied again and implemented in accord with the Church's teaching and practice as it has been handed down to us from the time of the Apostles.

By the time I was ordained in 1975 and assigned as assistant rector of the Cathedral of Saint Joseph the Workman in La Crosse, Wisconsin, I was shocked to discover that the devotional life of the Church had practically undergone a total devastation. There were no Eucharistic devotions, apart from, of course, the important form of visits to the Blessed Sacrament. I visited the homes of parishioners and discovered that there were no longer any sacred objects in the home. It was very infrequent to find a family which was praying the Rosary. In some homes, there were no longer prayers before and after meals. I was also involved in the Catholic schools, and I discovered that there, too, the devotional life had disappeared. This was a cause of great concern to me.

As a priest, I attempted to do what I could to reintroduce the devotional life because it is impossible to have a strong relationship with Our Lord, as we do most perfectly and fully through the Sacred Liturgy, above all through the Holy Eucharist, our participation in the Holy Sacrifice of the Mass and our encounter with Him in confession, that does not find its expression in acts of devotion throughout the day and in the various places in which we find ourselves. Somehow, in a kind of mistaken notion, after the Second Vatican Ecumenical Council, it was thought that the only way you could express your love of the Lord is through the Sacred Liturgy.

The Sacred Liturgy, of course, is the fullest and most perfect expression, but that is an expression which is offered in those very central moments of our life but cannot be done throughout the day in our homes, at work, at study, at recreation, and in our other human endeavors. Because of the intensity of the liturgical encounter and, especially, our love of the Holy Eucharist, we want to bring the reality of that encounter into our homes and other familiar places. We do this with sacred images, with prayers and with other special devotions. Yet as a priest, I was able to do a little to address the dearth of devotional life in the family.

On December 10, 1994, I was named Bishop of La Crosse. At that time, I began to reflect upon and pray about the pastoral needs of the whole Diocese, which were soon to become my principal care. Having grown up in the Diocese and having been ordained a priest for the Diocese, my reflection and prayer was filled with deepest affection for the people of the Diocese. When I was installed as the Eighth Bishop of La Crosse on February 22, 1995, I spoke about my pastoral concern for the family which has suffered so many assaults in our time. I also expressed concern about the violence which more and more marks our American culture.

In the face of the pastoral reality of living the Catholic faith in our time in the Diocese, I became more and more convinced of the need for a place of pilgrimage, an extraordinary place in the Diocese to which the faithful might come at any time, but especially in times of special joy and of special need to be renewed in faith and grace. I also came to understand that this place of pilgrimage should be dedicated to our Blessed Mother, the first and best among us who are the disciples of her Son, who constantly prays and works to draw us closer to the Redemption which her Son offers us in the Church. More specifically, in America, our Blessed Mother has shown forth the love and mercy of God the Father for all His children, especially those in most need, by her appearances at Tepeyac in 1531 to the faith-filled, humble native American, Saint Juan Diego and his uncle, Juan Bernardino.

Our Blessed Mother's appearances and message at Tepeyac show God's love and mercy as much to us today as she did almost 500 years ago. In fact, through the wonderful and scientifically unexplainable imprint of the image of Our Lady of Guadalupe on the mantle or *tilma* of Saint Juan Diego—the work of the hand of God—Our Lady continues to appear to those who come to venerate her at the place of her appearances in present-day Mexico City. It is a loving appearance and message for which we all hunger and which can draw us all to the fount of life and grace in our Lord Jesus Christ.

Then, in a Pastoral Letter in 1996, I announced that, as a preparation for the Great Jubilee of the Year 2000, and for the spiritual good of the faithful of our Diocese and of the faithful far beyond who seek to place their lives before the Lord in prayer and to receive from the Lord renewed faith and grace, I would establish in the Diocese a place of pilgrimage—a *shrine* dedicated to Our Lady, the Virgin Mother of God.

PRAYER, PLANNING, & LABOR

The Shrine was always intended to be dedicated to Our Lady because she really is the Mother of Devotion and, through her maternal guidance, all the other devotions come into place, including devotion to the Sacred Heart of Jesus, to the Blessed Sacrament, to the Passion of Our Lord, and to various saints. In the beginning, I thought to dedicate the Shrine to Our Lady of Fatima, in gratitude to her for saving Pope Saint John Paul II from the assassin's bullet on her feast day in 1981. That direction changed, however, when Pope John Paul II published his Post-Synodal Apostolic Exhortation, *Ecclesia in America,* "On the Encounter with the Living Jesus Christ: The Way to Conversion, Communion, and Solidarity in America," in which he underlined so strongly the apparitions and message of Our Lady of Guadalupe, and her love for the Church in America and his desire that devotion to her be fostered, not only in Central and South America, where it was already quite strong, but also in North America. Then I understood that the Shrine should be dedicated to Our Lady of Guadalupe.

I knew of her apparitions and message because we were taught the story of Our Lady of Guadalupe in Catholic elementary school, but in our home, we really did not know this apparition very well. Most people in the La Crosse Diocese had a great devotion to Our Lady of Lourdes (this was especially true in the home of my youth), so I began then to study intensely on the matter. It did not take long for me to realize that the miraculous events concerning the Virgin of Guadalupe constitute one of the most wonderful apparitions of Our Lady.

As soon as the work began for developing and planning and building the shrine, numerous difficulties also began. One of the first difficulties was to find the site upon which the shrine would be built. There was a site of a former cloistered Dominican convent in the City of La Crosse, which had been sold to a secular concern. I thought that the Lord was calling me to retrieve that convent and restore it as a shrine to Our Lady, but all my efforts in that regard failed. (We should never be surprised by such difficulties and failures: Anytime we want to do something good there is at least one person who is opposed; that is the Evil One, and he will be busy in his own subtle and attractive ways, sowing the seeds of confusion and division and error to hinder the progress of the work.)

Then, in 1997, two years after I was consecrated a bishop, I was attending an event at Aquinas High School in La Crosse when I was approached by Lucille Swing with her daughter, Jeanne Pavela née Swing. They invited me to inspect a property that Lucille's late husband, Robert, had purchased in 1950, shortly after he had returned home from serving our country in the Second World War. At the time, housing was in short supply, and Robert had been renting the upstairs of a home owned by a woman named Anna Betz, who sold the eggs from the chickens she raised on one hundred acres of land located on the south side of La Crosse. Mrs. Betz, who was no longer able to maintain the property and who greatly respected Robert, offered to sell him the house and the land for $10,000. (By the economic standards at the time of this writing in 2023, that would be over $1.2 million.) Robert cherished that rural land with its bucolic stream and hills; but, based on the salary he earned as an appliance salesman in town, he knew that he would not be able to afford such a purchase. Yet, despite any misgivings, he also accepted a deep sense of purpose that he had to do everything he could to buy that land. So, he asked friends for loans, he borrowed on a life insurance policy, and somehow, in the end, he raised enough funds to buy the house and the land—reminiscent of the joyfully determined man from Our Lord's parable in Matthew 13, 44: "The kingdom of heaven is like a treasure hidden in a field; he who finds it, hides it, and in his joy goes and sells all that he has and buys that field." Robert saw that the land itself was a treasure that he hoped would one day be developed for a religious purpose. He tried twice to donate the land, first to the Franciscan Sisters of Perpetual Adoration, and next to Viterbo University, but neither organization accepted his generous offer. Sadly, Robert passed away just two years before that momentous day when his wife Lucille approached me after the high school event and informed me that her family owned some beautiful land that might be the ideal place for founding a shrine. "If you would like it, we will give it to you," she said to me.

From the minute I laid eyes on the land, I felt what Robert Swing must have felt when he saw it. At that moment I realized that this land was the very place upon which the Shrine should be established.

When I announced the building of the Shrine, I had no idea of the amount of negative reaction I would receive. People said that it was a waste of money that should be spent on the poor and on Catholic education; that I was a scandal for doing this; that I was medieval, promoting an outdated notion; that no one would come to the shrine because it was simply out of step with the world today; that I was doing this to promote my own career in the Church, and all this kind of thing. Some of it was really quite dreadful. It got to the point that every morning, when I would come downstairs from my bedroom, there would be letters or an article or letter to the editor in the newspaper criticizing my efforts to develop the Shrine. I remember one letter to the editor said, "And then there will be a miracle, and then we will have chaos in the city." Some people said that shrines attract weird people and there will be crazy people coming to La Crosse and disturbing our peace. All kinds of primitive ideas were expressed.

Many obstacles were to be expected. But the Lord always sustained the work, and that is why I say it is His work. Without faith in Divine Providence, I surely would have given up on ever trying to accomplish such a work. From the beginning, Our Lord inspired devoted priests and lay faithful who generously worked with me in the planning and development of the Shrine.

From the early planning stages, Michael Swinghamer, a partner in the firm of River Architects, located in La Crosse, Wisconsin, was chosen as the principal architect on the project. It was an especially meaningful project for Michael since it was his uncle and aunt, Robert and Mary Lucille Swing, who donated the land; Michael played a key role in making their dreams a reality. Fowler & Hammer, a firm from La Crosse, Wisconsin, was chosen as the construction team. Jim Fowler, owner of the firm, and Mark Martell, project manager, worked closely with Michael Swinghamer and design consultant, Duncan G. Stroik, Architect LLC, of South Bend, Indiana, and professor at the University of Notre Dame School of Architecture. As will be noted later, Duncan Stroik was key to the design and appointment of a most beautiful classical church to serve Our Lady in her mission.

A key member of the Fowler & Hammer team was Gale Jesse, the construction superintendent. Gale was the vigilant supervisor of the construction project from the very first clearing of the ground, commuting an hour to work in all weather conditions and at all hours of the early morning and late evening. When others left work for the day, Gale could be seen giving a last look at cleanup of the site, checking blueprints for accuracy of execution, and generally ensuring that the work performed was of the highest quality. This team dedicated their talents for over four years, ensuring that even the smallest of details was not overlooked. They were just as diligent in their role of oversight of all subcontractors in the areas that will never be seen but which are central to the Shrine Church's ability to move us to prayer. Key subcontractors to this project came from all over Wisconsin and the United States. Locally based subcontractors that greatly aided the early stages of the Shrine Church's construction included geotechnical engineers at Chosen Valley Testing, civil engineers at Paragon Associates, Inc., and plumbing consultants at Shumann & Associates, Inc. Additional subcontractors brought from Madison, Wisconsin, include structural, HVAC, and fire protection consultants at Arnold & O'Sheridan, Inc., as well as landscape developers at Ken Saiki Design, Inc. Heebink Architectural Woodwork from Baldwin, Wisconsin, crafted the woodwork throughout the Shrine Church, including the ambo, pews, confessionals, and all the woodwork in the sacristies. The extraordinarily beautiful painting in the interior of the Church is the work of John Canning & Co. of Cheshire, Connecticut. The award-winning lighting and museum design firm, George Sexton Associates, from Washington, D.C., gave invaluable direction for proper lighting in the Shrine Church, while the lighting fixtures were supplied by Winona Lighting in Winona, Minnesota, supported by further direction from electrical consultants at Czarnecki Engineering, Inc. in Pewaukee, Wisconsin. Finally, providing incomparable designs for the interior of the Shrine Church's acoustics was the renowned acoustical design services of Robert F. Mahoney & Associates of Boulder, Colorado.

When the project had reached a point when we were ready to break ground, the first structure to be built was the place to receive pilgrims. One might think that the church ought to be built first, as the church is the goal of the pilgrimage; but you cannot just put up a church. The first two buildings to be established would be the Pilgrim Center as a place to offer hospitality to pilgrims and the Mother of Good Counsel Votive Candle Chapel as a place for devotion while the Shrine Church was being built. The Mother of Good Counsel Votive Candle Chapel continues to provide the possibility for the faithful, both those who come on pilgrimage and those who are not able to do so, to have candles burning for their many intentions.

The groundbreaking ceremony was held on the Feast of Our Lady of Fatima, May 13, 2004. Clearing began just two weeks before, with the construction team carefully toppling the fewest trees necessary for the building. But with unusually heavy rains, the site quickly turned to mud. Despite the heavy rains, we pushed ahead with the plans. The event was a success, with hundreds in attendance, including families with babies and buses with school children. Flanked by the Knights of Columbus, I presided over the groundbreaking ceremony and then led a Rosary procession to a statue of Our Lady of Guadalupe—the rain stopping just long enough for the crowning of the statue.

A year later, on May 19, 2005, we reached a major milestone when, in a special ceremony, I blessed the cornerstone of the church.

The inscription on the cornerstone reads:

"QUODCUMQUE DIXERIT VOBIS, FACITE"
(IO II, V)
ME BENEDIXIT ET POSUIT
RAIMUNDUS LEO BURKE
ARCHIEPISCOPUS SANCTI LUDOVICI DIE
XIX MAII A.D. MMV

This is translated:

"DO WHATEVER HE TELLS YOU" (JN 2, 5)
RAYMOND LEO BURKE
ARCHBISHOP OF ST. LOUIS
BLESSED AND PLACED ME ON MAY 19, 2005

From groundbreaking to dedication, building the Shrine Church was a massive undertaking. It would take 2,212 cubic yards of concrete, 119 tons of masonry and concrete reinforcing, 184 tons of structural steel, 93,831 concrete blocks, 664 tons of random stone, 900 tons of Indiana limestone, and 17,000 square feet of concrete tile roof to complete the Shrine Church. One of the great goals in all of the buildings is that we should strive to have them be of materials as beautiful as possible and also as enduring as possible. So, there was the continual need to raise funds. It would be a completely independent shrine. There was no money from the Diocese of La Crosse contributed to this work. It was all the work of the faithful who contributed to it. It was not a diocesan shrine; it was an independently constituted shrine, certainly under the direction of the hierarchy of the Church, but done completely as an act of devotion of the faithful.

As the Shrine Church was being built, I heard it said that, up to that time in the last fifty years, this was the first Catholic church in America to be built in a classical style. Architect Duncan Stroik was key to the design and decoration of the interior of the Shrine Church, for which he drew upon years of study of classical church architecture. Meticulous care was taken in the choice of materials, in their design, and in the various forms of the iconography—statues, paintings, friezes, frescos, inscriptions, etc.

The construction of the Shrine Church was finished in about four years. Sister Christa Marie Halligan, F.S.G.M., was the Executive Director of the Shrine during the years of construction. She helped me to direct and follow closely the entire work, especially after my transfer to the Archdiocese of Saint Louis, which was effective on January 26, 2004, the day of my installation as Archbishop of Saint Louis.

The Solemn Dedication of the Shrine Church was a cause of great joy; it marked the end of a long period of prayer, physical labor, and planning by many. The Dedication took place on July 31, 2008—the sixth anniversary of the canonization of Saint Juan Diego. Numerous guests were in attendance, including His Eminence Francis Cardinal George, O.M.I., His Eminence Justin Cardinal Rigali, over 20 Archbishops and Bishops, over 100 Priests, over 60 Knights and Ladies of the Holy Sepulchre, over 25 Knights of Columbus Honor Guard, members of the Saint Juan Diego—now the Saint José Sánchez del Río—Guild for Children, members of Marian Catechetical Apostolate, devoted faithful, benefactors, staff, volunteers, and friends, and over 1,000 pilgrims.

At the start of the ceremony, the doors to the Shrine Church were locked and those in attendance stood outside. When the doors were unlocked and the attendees entered, the altar was bare. It was not until after I had blessed the altar with holy water and anointed it with the Sacred Chrism that it had become set apart for sacred use. The Rite concluded with the offering of the Holy Sacrifice of the Mass, a fitting way to commence the Shrine's work in the sacramental mission of the Church.

One might think that, on the day of the Dedication of the Church on July 31, 2008, the work was accomplished. It was, in a certain sense; but then there remained the commitment to maintain the beauty, to make sure that the Shrine Church continued to serve as the heart of the Shrine and to inspire in the faithful a more intense encounter with Christ and a more fervent love of Him. When people come on a pilgrimage, they should come to a place which represents the great beauty and enduring—indeed, eternal—quality of our life in Christ. This Shrine was built at great sacrifice in order that it would be a truly beautiful place. So, whenever I am at the Shrine, I remind the staff and say to them, "The Shrine is a very beautiful place. But every day that we do not care for it attentively, it becomes less beautiful."

There is yet work to be done to complete the Shrine Church. Designs have been prepared for the Stations of the Cross, and the plans are ready for the completion of the Crypt which is temporarily being used as a place for presentations and meals. Once the Saint Juan Diego Retreat House, with its second floor which provides one large and two smaller rooms for presentations and meals, is built, the Crypt will be completed with an additional main altar and with side altars dedicated to various saints, for instance, Saint José Sánchez del Río and Blessed Carlo Acutis.

Today, the Shrine of Our Lady of Guadalupe is a privileged place built not merely with wood and stones, metal and mortar, but also built upon the immeasurable and enduring truth, goodness and beauty of Christ, which is made visible to us in the Sacred Liturgy, above all, in the offering of the Holy Sacrifice of the Mass. The Shrine is a place in which pilgrims may contemplate, through the eyes of the Virgin Mary, the Mystery of the Redemptive Incarnation, the Mystery of Faith, the Mystery of God's unfathomable and unceasing love at work for us in the Church, the Mystical Body of Christ, His only-begotten Son. At the Shrine, Our Lady of Guadalupe draws our hearts to hers, so that she may direct us, with maternal love, to place our hearts completely, one with her Immaculate Heart, into the glorious pierced Heart of Jesus, God the Son and her Son. At the Shrine, Our Lady of Guadalupe teaches us obedience to God's will, the ever-attentive listening to His voice and the renunciation of false idols, which is our only way to happiness and peace during the days of our earthly pilgrimage, and finally and perfectly at the destination of our pilgrimage, the Kingdom of Heaven.

The PURPOSE *of* PILGRIMAGE

Pilgrimage to a shrine is probably the most ancient devotion and one of the most effective devotions in the history of the people of God in the Old Testament, in Our Lord's Public Ministry, and then in the great tradition of the Church. The people of the Old Testament and Our Lord Himself took part in the annual pilgrimage to the Temple in Jerusalem which was seen as a very privileged place of the encounter with God. (Cf. Lk 2, 41-42.) In His public ministry, Jesus made this pilgrimage to Jerusalem and spoke about it very explicitly as a pilgrimage to accomplish our Redemption. (Cf. Jn 2, 13; 5, 1; 10, 22; and 12, 12.) In the Church, of course, we have the richness of holy places, some places made holy by Our Lord's very presence in the Holy Land, Jerusalem and Bethlehem, and other places made holy by our Lord's Church in Rome where Saints Peter and Paul were martyred for the faith, and then, from Rome, to numerous other holy places. Also, we have holy places in our own country, even in our very neighborhoods. For instance, in St. Louis, I had an early desire to make a pilgrimage to Perryville, the place of the Shrine of the Miraculous Medal, and also the place of the first foundations of those holy Vincentian Fathers who had so much to do with the establishment of the Catholic Church in Saint Louis, and also to the tomb of Saint Rose Philippine Duchesne, the heroic member of the Religious of the Sacred Heart of Jesus who left her homeland of France to teach the faith in America, especially to the Native Americans. Wisconsin has a richness of holy places and shrines, to which to go on pilgrimage, for example, Holy Hill, the National Shrine of Mary, Help of Christians, at

Hubertus, Wisconsin, and the Shrine of Our Lady of Good Help (Our Lady of Champion) at Champion, Wisconsin, made holy by the apparition of the Mother of God to Adele Brise in October of 1859.

This whole notion of shrine and pilgrimage was very much underlined by Pope Saint John Paul II as he was preparing us for the Great Jubilee in 2000. He did that over three years: 1997, 1998 and 1999, writing to us, on each of those years, about one of the Persons of the Holy Trinity, but, at the same time, asking the Pontifical Council for the Pastoral Care of Migrants and Itinerant People to produce two documents. One, in its translation into English, is entitled The Pilgrimage in the Great Jubilee, approved for publication by Pope John Paul II on April 11, 1998, and published later that month on April 25. The other, in its English translation, is entitled *The Shrine: Memory, Presence and Prophecy of the Living God*, published on May 8, 1999. These are important documents which help us to understand the great grace that is given to us when we come on pilgrimage. This emphasis on shrine and pilgrimage in the Church practically coincided with my becoming a Bishop and coming to La Crosse as Bishop.

Allow me to provide a few brief quotations on the importance of shrines in the pilgrimage experience from *The Pilgrimage in the Great Jubilee*:

> Pilgrimages symbolize the experience of the homo viator who sets out, as soon as he leaves the maternal womb, on his journey through the time and space of his existence. (no. 43)

All of us are traveling, even if we are not leaving our home, because we are going day by day toward our meeting with the Lord in death. We are not on this earth to stay. We are travelers.

> This is the fundamental experience of Israel which is marching toward the promised land of salvation and of full freedom; the experience of Christ who rose to heaven from the land of Jerusalem. (no. 43)

Christ makes that final pilgrimage to the Temple and there consummates our Redemption by His Passion, Death and Resurrection,

> thus opening the way toward the Father; the experience of the Church which moves on through history toward the heavenly Jerusalem; the experience of the whole of humankind which tends toward hope and fullness...
>
> The Word of God and the Eucharist accompany us in this pilgrimage toward the heavenly Jerusalem, of which shrines are a visible and living sign. When we reach it, the gates of the kingdom will open, we will abandon the traveling attire and the staff of the pilgrim and we shall enter our house definitively "to stay with the Lord for ever" (1 Th 4:17). There he will be in our midst as "the one who serves" (Lk 22:27) and he will share our meal, side by side with us (cf. Rv 3:20). (no. 43).

The great image of Heaven is the Wedding Feast of the Lamb.

With that emphasis on the preparation for the Great Jubilee of the Year 2000 and on pilgrimage as a way to prepare for the Great Jubilee by helping us to discover anew the true nature of our life as pilgrims, Pope Saint John Paul II called us to recover in our own lives that sense of how extraordinary our ordinary life is because Christ has come to save us, Christ dwells in our hearts, He dwells with us in the Church, even as He dwells in the Shrine Church in the Blessed Sacrament and, at every Mass, comes down to our altar from Heaven from His glorious seat at the Father to make sacramentally present for us the Sacrifice of Calvary.

The heart of the new evangelization is best described in a rather small document of Saint John Paul II, written at the conclusion of the Great Jubilee Year, a document called *Novo Millennio Ineunte*, "At the Close of the Great Jubilee of the Year 2000." In it, there is a beautiful passage in which he states that we must rediscover the extraordinary nature of our ordinary Christian life, especially as it is manifested in the celebration of the Sacred Liturgy, the meeting of Heaven and earth (cf. *Novo Millennio Ineunte*, no. 31).

It should not surprise us that, in our time, and especially under the pastoral care of both Pope Saint John Paul II and Pope Benedict XVI, there has been a great renewal of liturgical piety, a desire that the Sacred Liturgy be carried out with the greatest possible beauty and care, so that we not lose sight that in the Sacred Liturgy it is God Himself who comes to meet us, that it is Christ Who acts in the Sacred Liturgy. Thanks be to God, there is a renewal today to restore the sacred. It is needed so that we do not lose sight of the reality of God dwelling with us. It is an objective reality. It is not a figment of our minds, it is not something we are imagining. God Himself, our Lord Jesus Christ, gave us, for instance, the Holy Eucharist at the Last Supper and He gave us the essential form for the celebration. Down the centuries there has been development in the form of the rite, but always in continuity, pointing to the truth of the Holy Eucharist. The Church treasures, in particular, the form of the Roman Rite which has its origins during the time of Pope Saint Gregory the Great and ultimately in the time of the Apostles. Since the Second Vatican Ecumenical Council, with the changes it introduced in the form of the Roman Rite, it is known as the Usus Antiquior, the More Ancient Usage of the Roman Rite.

The integrity of our Christian life necessarily flows from our encounter with Our Lord in the Sacred Liturgy, especially in the Holy Eucharist and the Sacrament of Penance and then our deepening knowledge of that encounter through our study of the faith, our prayer, and our devotion. A small passage from the document on the shrine that I mentioned earlier, published in 1999, said:

> The "mystery of the temple" thus offers a wealth of possibilities for meditation and fruitful activity. (no. 17)

The temple is in a special way, the Shrine Church with the liturgical encounter with Christ. The Church is the heart of the pilgrimage to the Shrine. Perhaps one of the most effective meditations during your time here would be simply on the Church as it is physically represented here in this building. There are three elements described in no. 17 of the document, *The Shrine: Memory, Presence and Prophecy of the Living God*:

As a *memory* of our origin.

I do not think there is ever any time that we enter into a church when we are not reminded of our birth and of our parents, or, if we were baptized as adults, our entrance into the Church through Baptism, Confirmation, and First Holy Communion.

> The Shrine calls to mind God's initiative and helps pilgrims to recognize it with a sense of awe, gratitude and commitment.

It is too easy in our lives to take for granted the great signs of God's love for us, above all, in the Sacraments. A pilgrimage helps us to purify ourselves of that complacency and to renew in us the sense of wonder. Then also the church

As a place of the *divine presence*.

It is not simply reminding us of all those events, but we recognize that Christ is present here now, most of all in the Holy Eucharist reposed in the tabernacle, the Sacred Host, which is the Body, Blood, Soul and Divinity of Christ. We experience the source of that presence during the Holy Mass when Our Lord, through the ministry of our priests, comes into our midst to renew the Sacrifice on Calvary, and also in the presence of the priests who are hearing our confessions and in all of their ministrations. So the document says that as a place of divine presence

> it bears witness to God's faithfulness and his constant activity in the midst of his people, through his Word and the sacraments. (no. 17)

At the Shrine of Our Lady of Guadalupe, the principal image of Our Lady is behind the altar for a very distinct reason: because Our Lady is constantly drawing us to her Son. The paradigmatic image of this is the Wedding Feast at Cana at which Our Lord, with His disciples and His Mother, is present, when the newlyweds run out of wine. Mary, in the account, is very straightforward. She does not have any hesitation when the wine stewards become aware of the situation: she takes them to her Son and tells them, "Do whatever He tells you" (John 2, 5). Her response is paradigmatic for us: Our Lady is bringing us here, she brings us to the altar and to the tabernacle and to confession, also. She brings us to a fuller life in the Church. That was her message to Saint Juan Diego.

I invite you to read the little account of Our Lady's apparitions to Saint Juan Diego, the *Nican Mopohua*, as it was recorded by the Native American scholar Antonio Valeriano, who knew Saint Juan Diego and heard him repeatedly recount the apparitions and message of our Blessed Mother. Everything is about her showing to her children the mercy of God, which is most known to us in the Holy Eucharist and also in the Sacrament of Penance, in short, through our life in the Church.

We have memory, presence, and then the third aspect is prophecy.

> As a prophecy, or a reminder of our heavenly homeland, it makes us remember that everything is not finished, but must yet be accomplished fully in accordance with God's promise which is our goal. (no. 17)

The wonderful thing about a pilgrimage, if we have been sort of "drifting along" in life, is that it reminds us that we indeed are on a journey. It is not some aimless journey, but it has a very specific direction for the final encounter with Our Lord. We are preparing for that encounter every day of our lives.

I always remember that at home and then in school we were taught to pray for a holy death. I said that to someone once, and he said, "Was that not very morbid?" And I said, "No, not at all. We did not think that there was anything strange about it, because it is good for us, even from the time we are small, to know that we are on a journey which will end in death, which is not the end for us, but really the fulfilment." A pilgrimage is prophetic in that way, in reminding us of our final destiny and that we have a lot to do yet to prepare to meet the Lord. Even if we are older, our work is not done in terms of our prayer and sacrifices and whatever else the Lord asks us to do. Sometimes even when we are older, we encounter great difficulties in the family or among friends that require special acts of love on our part. The pilgrimage prepares us to be ready for all those circumstances.

> Precisely by showing the relativity of everything penultimate in regard to our ultimate homeland, shrines point to Christ as the new Temple of mankind reconciled with God. (no. 17)

DEVOTION *to* MARY

Before describing further the specific devotion to Our Lady of Guadalupe, allow me to share a few general remarks on devotion to the Blessed Virgin Mary.

Devotions are prayers and practices by which we strive to express our love of God and deepen our participation in the mystery of the Redemptive Incarnation. For instance, devotion to the Most Sacred Heart of Jesus deepens our understanding of the infinite love of God for us, manifest in the Heart of the Incarnate Son of God, and leads us to a fuller participation in the Holy Eucharist in which our Lord Jesus offers His very life to us under the species of bread and wine. In this sense, as Pope Pius XI taught so well in his Encyclical Letter, *Miserentissimus Redemptor* (May 8, 1928), the devotion to the Sacred Heart of Jesus is the summit of all devotion.

Devotions also inspire us to express the love of God in our homes and in all our relationships. Devotions are words and actions which express devotion or love for God or for one of His saints. Among the saints, Mary is the first and the best, and so devotions to her have marked the life of the Church from the moment when Our Lord Jesus, dying on the cross for our salvation, gave her as mother to the Apostle John—representing the entire Church of all time and every place—and confided her to the care of the Apostle John as her son (cf. Jn 19, 26-27).

Devotion to our Blessed Mother deepens within us our understanding of the mystery of the Redemptive Incarnation and leads us to fuller union with the Incarnate Redeemer. As disciples of Our Lord Jesus, we are naturally drawn to

His Mother who was the first to welcome the Redeemer into the world, when she responded, "Let it be done to me as you say" to the Archangel Gabriel's announcement that she was to conceive the Redeemer in her womb by the power of the Holy Spirit (Lk 1, 38). From the moment of the Incarnation of the Redeemer in the Virgin Mary's womb to the moment of the Redeemer's death on the cross, Mary steadfastly embraced God's will for her Son and for her, even when it was difficult to understand and when it entailed the acceptance of intense suffering and even death. Mary's perfect discipleship is reflected in her words to the table waiters at the Wedding Feast of Cana, whom, in their distress, she took to her Divine Son with the clear and loving maternal counsel: "Do whatever He tells you" (Jn 2, 5).

Mary is always leading us to a closer following of Christ, a fuller love of Him. Pope John Paul II stated so clearly the meaning of Marian devotion in his Post-synodal Apostolic Exhortation *Ecclesia in America* ("The Church in America"), promulgated on January 22, 1999 at the Shrine of Our Lady of Guadalupe in Mexico City:

> Devotion to the Mother of the Lord, when it is genuine, is always an impetus to a life guided by the spirit and truths of the Gospel (no. 11).

Pope Paul VI reflected the same truth in his Apostolic Exhortation *Marialis Cultus* ("For the Right Ordering and Development of Devotion to the Blessed Virgin Mary") of February 2. 1974:

> Devotion to the Mother of the Lord becomes for the faithful an opportunity

> for growing in divine grace, and this is the ultimate aim of all pastoral activity. For it is impossible to honor her who is full of grace (Lk 1,28) without thereby honoring in oneself the state of grace, which is friendship with God, communion with Him and the indwelling of the Holy Spirit (no. 57).

Through devotion to the Ever-Virgin Mary, Our Blessed Mother inspires us and accompanies us in the renewal of our covenant of love with our Lord. Given to us as our Mother by her Divine Son, the ever-Virgin Mary draws us with maternal love to her Immaculate Heart, under which God the Son took a human heart. She leads us to place our hearts, with her Immaculate Heart, totally into His Sacred Heart—the only source of truth, goodness and beauty.

DEVOTION *to* OUR LADY *of* GUADALUPE

On the American continent—North America, Central America, and South America—, Marian devotion is frequently centered around the figure of our Blessed Mother as she appeared in December of 1531 to the Native American, Saint Juan Diego, at Tepeyac Hill in the area of modern-day Mexico City. Our Blessed Mother actually appeared four times to him and once to his dying elderly uncle, Juan Bernardino. The fourth appearance to Saint Juan Diego was the most wonderful. A brief account of the apparitions will help us to appreciate better God the Father's purpose in sending the Blessed Mother to us at Tepeyac and the important meaning of devotion to Our Lady of Guadalupe.

The first apparition took place on December 9, which at that time was the Solemnity of the Immaculate Conception in the Spanish Empire, of which Mexico was then a part. Our Blessed Mother appeared to Saint Juan Diego, an older native American who had recently lost his dear wife. Juan Diego was a devout Catholic but a man of no particular prominence in the local society or the Church. He had been living with and looking after his elderly uncle, Juan Bernardino, who was gravely ill. Juan Diego was on his way to church to participate in the Mass for the Solemnity of the Immaculate Conception and in the catechetical instruction given by the Franciscan friars, which followed the Holy Mass. As he reached Tepeyac Hill, he heard beautiful music and a beautiful voice calling out his name. Our Blessed

Mother appeared to him as the "woman clothed with the sun" of chapter 12 of the *Book of Revelation*, pregnant with the Child Jesus. She instructed Juan Diego to go to the house of Bishop Juan de Zumárraga and to request that a chapel be built in her honor on Tepeyac Hill so that she might show the infinite majesty and mercy of God to all His children of America and indeed to all His children.

Juan Diego went to the Bishop's house, where he was received with great respect but also with hesitation regarding his story of the apparition and of our Blessed Mother's request. The Bishop, who was praying and working to bring together the native Americans and the Spanish conquerors and settlers, requested time to consider the matter.

On Juan Diego's return home, the Blessed Mother appeared to him for the second time. Disappointed that he had failed in his mission, he asked Our Lady of Guadalupe to send a more esteemed messenger to the Bishop, so that he would believe the message. Our Blessed Mother instructed Juan Diego to return to the Bishop with her request.

The third apparition took place on December 10. Juan Diego had gone to the Bishop for a second time. The Bishop responded by asking for a sign so that he might believe the Blessed Mother's request. On his way home, Our Lady of Guadalupe appeared to Juan Diego, and he told her of the Bishop's request of a sign. Our Lady promised to provide the sign for the Bishop when Juan Diego would return to her on the next day.

Juan Diego missed his appointment with Our Lady of Guadalupe on December 11 because he was looking after his uncle Juan Bernardino who was gravely ill. On December 12, he was hurrying to bring a priest to administer the sacraments to his uncle who was dying. He took a different route in order to avoid another encounter with the Blessed

Mother, embarrassed that he had missed the appointment on December 11 and not wanting to be delayed in seeking spiritual help for his uncle.

Our Lady of Guadalupe appeared to him nonetheless, assuring him that his uncle was already cured and instructing him to gather flowers on the top of the hill as a sign to take to the Bishop. Juan Diego trusted Our Lady and found on the top of the frozen and barren hill the most beautiful flowers. He gathered them and Our Blessed Mother arranged them in his cloak or *tilma* as it was called. Juan Diego then hurried to the Bishop's house where this fourth apparition reached its fullness. When he opened his tilma to show the flowers to the Bishop, Our Lady of Guadalupe appeared depicted on the tilma. The Bishop immediately understood the truth of Juan Diego's message from the Blessed Mother and hastened to have the chapel built on Tepeyac Hill. In fact, on December 26, 1531, the sacred tilma was solemnly transferred to the chapel. The solemn transfer was also the occasion of the first miracle associated with the sacred image of Our Lady of Guadalupe.

The fifth apparition took place in the little home in which Juan Diego was living with his uncle. At the same time of her fourth apparition to Saint Juan Diego, Our Lady of Guadalupe appeared to Juan Bernardino and cured him of his fatal illness. She also revealed to Juan Bernardino the title by which she wished to be called: Our Lady of Guadalupe. Juan Diego himself died in 1548, seventeen years after the apparitions, at the age of 74. On May 6, 1990, Pope Saint John Paul II, during his second pilgrimage as Pope to the Shrine of Our Lady of Guadalupe, declared Juan Diego blessed. On July 31, 2002, Pope Saint John Paul II presided at his canonization in the Basilica of Our Lady of Guadalupe in Mexico City.

It should come as no surprise to us that, once the chapel was built and the people responded to Our Lady's invitation to visit her there, so that she might manifest God's mercy and love to them, there was a transformation of the culture of death which prevailed at the time. The cruel and truly demonic practice of massive human sacrifice among the Aztec people ceased. The inhuman treatment of the native Americans by the Spanish explorers and settlers also ceased. Coming to Our Lady, the people experienced the truth that God the Son was incarnate in her womb, that He came to us in our human flesh, in order to save us from our sins and eternal death by His Passion, Death, Resurrection and Ascension, and that He continues to be alive for us in the Church, pouring forth without measure and without cease, the sevenfold grace of the Holy Spirit into our hearts from His glorious pierced Heart. Truly, the divine light of heaven shown upon earth, enlightening and strengthening the people coming on pilgrimage to live a God-fearing life and to offer loving worship to God.

Today, offering devotion to Our Blessed Mother by coming on pilgrimage to the Shrine of Our Lady of Guadalupe, it is important to reflect in a particular way upon the essential relationship between sacred worship and right conduct in our daily living. Our Lady appeared to Saint Juan Diego, asking that the Bishop build a chapel, a place of worship of God "in spirit and truth" (Jn 4, 23-24.) The chapel, in which she was to be present in a privileged way, was to be the place of encounter with the immeasurable and unceasing mercy and love of God towards all men, most especially through the Sacraments of Penance and the Holy Eucharist.

Pray that your pilgrimage to visit Our Lady of Guadalupe today will enlighten and strengthen you to put God first in your lives, to put prayer and the worship of God in the first place of your activities, so that His truth and love may enlighten every aspect of your lives.

ARRIVING AT THE SHRINE

As pilgrims arrive at the Shrine, they are greeted by two statues.

The first is a statue of Saint Juan Diego donated by His Eminence Cardinal Norberto Rivera Carrera, then Archbishop of Mexico City, to the Shrine on the occasion of the Solemn Dedication of the Shrine Church on July 31, 2008. This statue, which depicts Saint Juan Diego holding open his tilma upon which is the miraculous image of Our Lady of Guadalupe, is located at the juncture of the Shrine's parking lot and the walkway leading to the Pilgrim Center. The second statue is of Our Lady of Guadalupe in the plaza before the entrance to the Pilgrim Center. Commissioned in 2001 by the Shrine, this magnificent statue of Our Lady was created by the artist Enrique de la Vega and, in the following year, the statue was installed after the completion of the Pilgrim Center. Today, the statue stands in the plaza of the Pilgrim Center, facing the entryway, greeting pilgrims as they arrive and, as they return home, offering a last visual representation of Our Lady's maternal love experienced at the Shrine.

Read more about the Shrine in Cardinal Burke's book ***The Shrine of Our Lady of Guadalupe****.*

shrine.now/shrine-book

Make a pilgrimage to the Shrine of Our Lady of Guadalupe.

guadalupeshrine.org

cardinalburke.com

www.ingramcontent.com/pod-product-compliance
Lightning Source LLC
LaVergne TN
LVHW091145080826
845145LV00008B/2263